CONTENTS

The Security of South-East Asia

INTRODUCTION

Does South-east Asia need to have new forms of security?

The old forms still exist, but as a ragbag of discards which may survive for a while for reasons of convenience or neglect, but cannot be taken seriously in the long term. Moreover, it is possible that interesting and perhaps unique conditions are present in South-east Asia, which will reward a quite different analysis from that which brought about the security arrangements of the 1950s and 1960s. There is at present a stand-off among the external powers, and a local movement has developed in support of self-reliance, both national and regional. South-east Asia is, therefore, at an important stage of its post-colonial development, in that, for the first time in its history, it may be able to forestall dominance by one or a number of external powers.

The obstacles are impressive, not the least being that South-east Asia can hardly be said to exist as a 'region'. It does not appear to have either the political will or the cohesion to act in a sufficiently determined and sophisticated way to impress on the external powers the wisdom of non-intervention. Indeed, the dramatic end to the Vietnam War has introduced new elements of uncertainty into the relations of local states with each other, so that what seemed to be a consensus against intervention when the American commitment in Vietnam was demonstrably failing is now not so easily aroused.

However, it is an axiom of international relations, or should be, that every action does not have an equal and opposite reaction; one does not have to produce a codified regional proposal on non-interference in order to stimulate a response from the external powers. They could conclude, without discussing the matter among themselves, that non-intervention has its own attractions for each of them. It is possible that forms of security will develop from individual, disparate and even conflicting responses, occurring both within the area and also outside it.

It is the purpose of this Paper to explore this possibility. I am aware of both dangers and opportunities and am concerned to minimize neither. The note of urgency which again marks the study of security in South-east Asia reflects the unsettling effect of the shift of power to Vietnam. It is also a response to the prospect that, while Vietnam is pre-occupied with restoring a war-ravaged economy, and while the external powers are contemplating the tantalizing possibility that they need not, after all, be hostile to each other in this part of the world, an opportunity exists to find forms of security for South-east Asia which will be more constructive and more enduring than those of the past.

One fact stands out. None of the great powers now has a major military presence in South-east Asia and there is not, as yet, an arms race within the region. If attention is paid to the security of South-east Asia at this stage, the chances are greater that the issues can be resolved at a low, rather than a high, level of forces.

Since 1975, when Vietnam was unified by force of arms, a shift of power has occurred in the region. One aspect of this is the fact of Vietnam itself. She is militarily strong, politically confident, ideologically combative, and she has a history of nationalism. She sees herself as playing a significant role in future developments in South-east Asia.

Another aspect is that there is at present no apparent military counter or balance to Vietnam. Vietnam's armed forces are now roughly the equal of those of all non-Communist South-east Asian countries combined.[1] Even allowing for the fact that the spoils of war look more impressive on paper than on the ground, especially in a few years' time when the lack of spare parts becomes apparent,[2] Vietnam has shown herself to be resourceful in military matters, and her forces are experienced and tough. She must now be regarded as the major military power in South-east Asia. While her intentions and motivations are important and must be carefully assessed, it would be flying in the face of the known behaviour of nation states and the experience of conflict not to be concerned by the absence of any structure (or even consensus) in the region which might act as a deterrent or a constraint should Vietnam wish to act militarily.

Security Arrangements in South-East Asia

Remnants of earlier security arrangements remain, without cohesion or, indeed, coherence. The South-East Asia Collective Defence Treaty (1954) remains on paper, but the South-East Asia Treaty Organization (SEATO), its military component, has been disbanded. Its membership has collapsed and its anti-Communist objectives, always confusing, have now become irrelevant.[3] The Asian and Pacific Council (ASPAC), formed in 1966, was political in conception, and some hoped it might be the beginning of a wider regional security arrangement. It is now dormant and, because it includes Taiwan, is unlikely to be revived.

The ANZUS Treaty (1951) remains active, but as its members comprise only Australia, New Zealand and the United States, and as its vaguely defined theatre ('the Pacific area') has tended, at least in the United States' interpretation, to exclude South-east Asia, it has no direct regional influence. The so-called five-power defence arrangement (1971) between Malaysia, Singapore, Britain, Australia and New Zealand remains in being, but both Britain and Australia have withdrawn their ground forces, and the arrangement's purely Commonwealth nature and its stopgap character severely limit its regional application. Indeed, it has sometimes seemed pre-occupied with keeping Singapore and Malaysia on sensible terms. It is notable that Britain maintains forces in Brunei. The United States has almost completely withdrawn her forces from Thailand and is in the process of negotiating terms for retaining her bases in the Philippines, with whom she has a bilateral security treaty, the only one in South-east Asia.

The Association of South-East Asian Nations (ASEAN), formed in 1967, is the most substantial regional grouping which offers some kind of counter to Vietnam. It has been slow to develop, but it includes five important states (Thailand, Malaysia, Singapore, Indonesia and the Philippines) and has shown some skill in creating a consensus on foreign-policy issues. Its economic and cultural co-operation remains low-key, however, its regional organization has little status or authority, and it has deliberately avoided security decisions itself, although it has encouraged security co-operation among its members. The ASEAN states have taken the view that economic development is the most effective form of security, and the biggest and most important of them – Indonesia – has deliberately starved her armed forces, especially her navy and air force, of scarce foreign exchange. While its potential is strong, ASEAN is still in two minds about its future as a security arrangement.

The security arrangements that remain in South-east Asia today are the left-overs of the Anglo-American ascendancy; they are ineffectual, yet give rise to the suspicion that they could be revived.

The Example of Vietnam: A Pattern for the Future?

There is also a symbolic aspect to Vietnam's strength, which is that the Vietnamese are heroes of history. Every nation has its heroes, but the Vietnamese in power today in Hanoi must rank high on any list of heroes, especially in South-east Asia where, with the exception of the Indonesians who removed the Dutch by a combination of armed resistance and active diplomacy, the existing nation states had a comparatively easy road to independence. The Vietnam War, the longest and bloodiest of all wars of national independence since the colonial era began to crumble after World War II, resulted not only in the success of the Vietnamese Communists, but in the first military defeat of the United States and in a major reversal of American foreign policy. The consequences of this are still not clear. To some extent the rethinking of American foreign policy since 1969, when the commitment in Vietnam began to be reversed, was prolonged by the discrediting of President Nixon and the interim leadership of President Ford, and it is only since the the installation of a new President in 1977 that the future outline of American policy in the Asian-Pacific region has begun to emerge. It is possible that the heroic stature of Vietnam may act as a source of national fulfilment, rather than as a spur to further demonstrations of her prowess. But for the other states of South-east Asia, which had been growing accustomed to the long, slow, pragmatic process of con-solidating independence after the transfer of sovereign political power, the emergence of a vital, confident, new state, freshly successful from a classic colonial war, has caused appre-hension and self-examination. In addition, it may be that the profounder effects of the defeat in Vietnam on United States policy have not yet emerged.

There is a widespread view that South-east Asia will 'settle down' or 'right itself' in time. It is held that the region is capable, with its porous borders, passive populations and strong governments, of absorbing shocks and accom-modating itself to conditions of not-too-efficient survival. One should not think of South-east Asians as constituting nation states. Rather, their ties are more strongly with race, family and commerce. They are fated (doomed or privileged, according to taste) to have a low profile in international affairs because they acquiesce willingly to international forces, whether religious, political or commercial. This view, however, puts too low a value on nationalism to provide a useful guide to future

events. For the state is no less powerful in South-east Asian countries than elsewhere and, whether in the policing of internal security or in the protection of territorial integrity, it has shown itself to be as self-conscious as any. In the last ten years South-east Asian nationalism has indeed been low-key. The Vietnam War was the dominant issue of those ten years, and political nationalism in the region was subdued, not only by the determining strategic effect of the war but also by the profits which flowed from it. But the arrival of a united Vietnam on the scene will (with other factors)[4] stimulate the latent nationalism, which never lies very far beneath the surface in South-east Asian politics.

The shift of power to Vietnam has raised afresh the problem of Communist insurgency in South-east Asia. In both Thailand and Malaysia Communist insurgency has been increasing recently, and the success of the Vietnamese troops in guerrilla warfare (like that of the Chinese Communists before them) will no doubt inspire confidence in the strategy of insurgency. Yet the assumption that Vietnam is the model for revolutionary guerrilla warfare in other countries of South-east Asia would be just as much a mistake now as it was in the 1960s. As will be seen, her problems are different. More-over, it is worth recalling that, so far, Communist insurgency in South-east Asia has not been successful, with the exception of Vietnam. The uniqueness of Vietnam, which made her a model of successful defiance of all the arts of counter-insurgency that money could buy, lay in the distinctive combination of nationalism and Communism which gave her revolution par-ticular force. The Viet Minh were the patriots, Ho Chi Minh was the father of the nation, and France and the United States, trying to build an alternative nationalism around other leaders in the south, were opposing Vietnamese nation-alism. In the rest of South-east Asia the situation was reversed. The departing colonial powers gave authority to the nationalists, and the Communists had to attempt to seize power from nationalist leaders, which they failed to do. It is, therefore, unlikely that the brilliant Vietnamese victory will be repeated elsewhere in South-east Asia, always provided that the performance of nationalist governments can be maintained.

3

Equilibrium: Practical Alternative to Hegemony?
The notion of a shift of power to Vietnam may seem to pre-suppose that a balance of power should be brought into existence to correct it. However, the concept of a balance of power does not readily fit the known dispositions of either the states within the region or the powers external to it.[5] If history is a guide, petty rivalry within the region and external hegemony or pervasive penetration from outside is a more likely pattern. The famous balance-of-power system which maintained conditions of relative peace in nineteenth-century Europe (even if it did not preserve internal peace, as witness the uprisings of 1848 and 1870) was upheld by resident actors who were not themselves subject to major pressures from outside Europe. In South-east Asia the resident states, such as they are, have not traditionally been the objects of a power balance in the region, let alone the focus of a concert of powers. To the extent that they have been subject to the exigencies of their foreign relations, they have been rivals skirmishing for minor advantages under the broad influence of outside forces, whether the cultural and trading stimulus of India, the tributary system of China, the domination of the European colonial powers, the Japanese 'Co-Prosperity Sphere' or the United States' strategy of containing Communism.

Strategic power can change the course of history. The long period of colonialism did not, however, for it merely divided South-east Asia along different lines, so that the Asian states become proxy rivals for their metropolitan powers: Indonesia looking to Holland; Indo-China to France; Singapore, Malaysia and Burma to Britain; and the Philippines to Spain and then to the United States. The later attempts of the United States to fuse the regional states into a bloc united in opposition to China (and to Communism) failed because some of the most significant states – Indonesia, Malaysia and Singapore (not to mention India, if we go as far afield as Pakistan for one new nation which *did* respond) – declined to join. The result was that no tradition of regional response has emerged to replace the waning, discredited tradition of hegemony.

Nor is there an external balance of power which might hover benevolently over South-east Asia, while the connective tissues of regional co-operation were formed. The great powers are disengaged at present, but their interests are so divergent that it is difficult to be confident that there exists between them a 'field' of unity which could be exploited to create equilibrium. The prospect of a balance of power in South-east Asia has intrigued observers, since in proclaiming the Guam Doctrine in 1969, subsequently refined as the Nixon Doctrine in 1971, the United States has indicated that, while honouring her existing treaties and continuing to provide a nuclear shield, she could not be expected to support her allies with manpower in the event of conventional aggression or internal subversion. Writers have imaginatively constructed intersecting triangles of different qualities of power and have suspended mobiles with forces interacting at different levels and angles to demonstrate the variety of power and influence available in the major states concerned: the United States, the Soviet Union, China and Japan. However, while diplomatic unity is emerging among these four powers, in the sense that they perceive and treat each other more or less as equals, this consensus reflects, as yet, only a phase in their relations. The apparent abandonment of hostility between the United States and China, for example, has not yet been tested by new positions. In the absence of new policies or strategies, the four powers have adopted a wait-and-see attitude, without quite abandoning old policies or proposing new ones. What we have, in other words, is not so much a balance as a 'pause' or 'hiatus'.

It would seem unlikely, therefore, that the strategy of containment, as practised by the United States against China, can be transferred somehow to a lower gear for use against Vietnam, or that a regional balance of power, based on the shifting weight of a group of countries consciously rectifying imbalance, will emerge from the present circumstances of South-east Asia. The problem is one of relating an external balance, or the lack of it, to an internal balance, or the lack of it, bearing in mind also that security alliances in South-east Asia must deal more with political instability, subversion and territorial attrition than with identifying adversaries and offering a credible deterrent to them.

4

Thailand has always been the most sensitive of the ASEAN states to developments in Vietnam, and it is there that the first test of the security problem of what used to be called 'post-Vietnam' South-east Asia has occurred. The armed forces' coup of October 1976, which brought to an end three years of democratic government, may have been mainly a response to instability, social violence and administrative indecisiveness which alarmed the business community, rather than a direct response to the shift of power to Vietnam. However, the new government in Bangkok set about distinguishing its foreign policy from the well-meaning attempts by its democratic predecessors to reach out to the Communist leaders across the border. The anti-Communist rhetoric of the SEATO era was revived and, in particular, co-operation with Malaysia against Communist insurgents on the Thai-Malaysian border was stepped up. In his initial address to the nation, Prime Minister Thanin said Thailand would no longer 'kowtow' to countries which were unfriendly. He rejected the 'two-faced' attitudes of 'some countries in the Communist bloc' which tried to separate state and party relations, and stressed the need for Thailand to mend fences with her old friends, especially the United States, Japan and her fellow members of ASEAN. He criticized the former government for setting a deadline for the withdrawal of American forces from Thailand and, although agreeing that neither Thailand nor the United States wished to return to previous levels of military co-operation, he claimed: 'It is now time for the countries of the free world to rise up and stand side by side with each other in the struggle against the Communist imperialists.'[6] Several of his ministers took up the anti-Communist refrain, especially the Interior Minister, Samak Sundaravej, who disclosed dramatically that Vietnam was actually preparing an invasion of Thailand on three fronts (from Burma, Laos and Cambodia).[7] Most observers were sceptical about the early rhetoric and the drama. It seemed to them that Hanoi did not want trouble with her ASEAN neighbours, as she was anxiously courting international opinion in pursuit of loans and investment, and that Thai talk of the 'free world' was primarily aimed at reassuring American

and Japanese investors. While both Hanoi and Moscow were sharply critical of the new regime in Bangkok, little was heard initially from Peking and Phnom Penh. It was thought that, after a while, a form of co-existence between Thailand and her Communist neighbours would emerge.

However, during 1977 the historic hostility between Thailand and her eastern neighbours reasserted itself. Outbreaks of incidents on the borders of both Laos and Cambodia increased, protest notes were exchanged and propaganda stepped up. Hanoi reacted particularly vehemently to Bangkok reports of a combined offensive with Malaysia against insurgents in the South, when aircraft and artillery were used and extensive damage to the Communist forces claimed. The Vietnamese army paper *Quan Doi Nhan Dan*[8] claimed that the United States was returning to Thailand, which she had always considered a 'vital bridgehead' in her military strategy in the Pacific and South-east Asia. It said that the United States had publicized her military withdrawal from Thailand because her presence was unpopular both in Thailand and in the United States, but had really only 'taken a step back in order to prepare to take another step forward'. American air bases and tele-communications and electronic espionage bases were again being prepared 'to accommodate their former occupants when necessary, or they were still operating under the direct control of US advisers'. The United States was secretly maintaining 'Vang Pao's moribund jungle bandits', who had fled from Laos. The commentary predicted, in language which revived memories of the long war in Vietnam, that inevitably the forces of justice and liberation would inflict a heavy defeat on the American 'neo-colonialist aggressors'.

The language of propaganda is necessarily crude, and propaganda is itself sometimes a substitute for action. Yet the deterioration in relations between Thailand and the three former Indo-Chinese states was evident. It represented a set-back to the hope that the shift of power to Vietnam and the accession to government of Communists in Laos and Cambodia could be accommodated by tact and patience. The coup in Bangkok, representing the still unresolved nature of political society in Thailand, combined with the ideological commitment of the governments in Vietnam, Cambodia and Laos to produce a situation of conflict which may or may not be controllable but which will not resolve itself without effort.

This situation can be traced back to the American strategy of using Thailand as a forward base of containment, or, much further back, to historic rivalries. Whichever is the case, conflict has questionable benefits for Thailand. During the democratic interlude in Thailand in 1973-76, the United States attempted to recognize the new state of affairs on the Indo-China peninsula by easing Thailand back into her role before World War II of buffer state, because the neutral zone formerly provided, however imperfectly, by Laos and Cambodia had now been occupied by Communist forces. The attempt was made without calling into question Thailand's commitment to ASEAN and, indeed, formed part of a broad ASEAN strategy of improving relations with the Communist states of Asia, as was achieved with China from 1972 and with Vietnam, Laos and Cambodia during 1975. After the coup of October 1976 Thailand seemed to be projecting herself once again as an anti-Communist bulwark, but without any hope of gaining the support of the United States or even that of all her ASEAN partners.

Part of Thailand's concern has been specifically the growth of insurgency. The insurgency operations there, under the control of the Communist Party of Thailand (CPT), began in 1965 with a few hundred activists. Now they number more than 800 in three areas[9] – the north (mainly a revolt of hill tribesmen), the north-east (where economic and social conditions are poor and the insurgents are mainly ethnically Lao) and the south (where Thai Communists are active in some areas and Thai Moslem secessionists in others) – and across the border Chin Peng still harasses the Malaysian Government. The CPT was originally led mainly by Sino-Thais rather than ethnic Thais, and is backed by the 'Voice of the People of Thailand', a radio transmitter stationed in southern China. Most of the CPT's training and material support comes from Laos and Vietnam.

The movement has not yet developed a mass political base, but with the recent defection of students and intellectuals from Bangkok this

could grow, creating the conditions for civil war. In any case, a broad base is not necessary for the application of significant pressure, as was shown by the pressure exerted by Vietnam on political events in Laos during the 1960s. Vietnamese troops in Laos – now reported to be back to the level of about 40,000[10] – kept up the pressure. They could do the same in Thailand from sanctuaries in the north and north-east of the country, once these had been established.

However, while Thailand's concern is understandable, the country is not in a strong position to present herself as a 'bulwark', whatever the cause. Her weakness, which has been obscured in recent years by impressive growth rates, plentiful foreign exchange and a surplus of rice for export, lies in a failure to develop her rural hinterland. Her economic success has depended greatly on the historical accident of the Vietnam War and the inflow of aid and investment, but this has itself widened the gap between city and countryside. The insurgencies in north and north-east Thailand reflect the economic and social deprivation of these areas at least as much as the inadequacy of counter-insurgency techniques or the success of Communist propaganda. In the rise and fall of kingdoms on the periphery of mainland Asia, the loss of control by capitals over a disintegrating hinterland has been an essential factor, and Bangkok today, with its Western commercial outlook and rival bureaucratic-military-business élites, faces the prospect of disintegration. To turn Bangkok into another modern capital of industry and commerce may provide satisfactory economic statistics in the short term, but the venture will only encounter competition from other centres of industry and commerce in South-east Asia, and risks forcing the postponement of the long overdue concentration on rural development. This weakness provides Vietnam, Laos or Cambodia with a classic opportunity to exploit the internal divisions of Thailand, which have been heightened by the coup of October 1976, through the alienation of many of the youth and leftist elements, who supported the democratic experiment and the first, but growing, controversy over the monarchy.[11] By emphasizing the issue of security, based on the need for stability to protect foreign investment, rather than concentrating on political reconciliation and long-term rural improvements, Thailand may have played into the hands of her adversaries.[12]

The threat to Thailand is one of attrition, a product not of the activities of a conquering foreign army in Bangkok but of the loss of her northern border regions from the heartland of the Central Plain by the accession of 'liberated zones',[13] with the south possibly in a state of disorder which would endanger road and rail access to Malaysia and Singapore. The heartland could still survive under those circumstances, with Bangkok thriving at its centre, but the cost of the losses, in terms of both military budgets and political prestige, would cause political turmoil and, eventually, political change.

The security problem in Thailand, in other words, can be seen as long-term and primarily political and economic, rather than short-term and primarily military. The country has several strong political and economic advantages if her external relations can be moderated. She has never been colonized, a fact which has promoted national pride, and the monarchy has in the past provided a core of political stability. Also, Thailand is an exporter of rice. A political and economic course which exploited factors such as these, and which utilized Buddhist support for policies of internal reconciliation and external harmony rather than of confrontation within and without, would seem to be in Thailand's interests, but it is a course unlikely to be taken, unfortunately, while the army's entrenched interest in the country's politics is limited to the search for a strong man. Thailand's military importance to the United States for the last fifteen years or so has given the Thai army a political role which present circumstances no longer demand, unless an army leader can be found with a taste for sophisticated diplomacy and skill in promoting internal stability.

III. THE ASEAN STATES

Malaysia

In Malaysia there was a milder response to the changes in Indo-China, despite Hanoi's attacks at the non-aligned summit meeting in August 1976 on ASEAN and on Malaysia's plan for a zone of peace, friendship and neutrality in South-east Asia (see page 24). Under the prime ministership of the late Tun Razak, Malaysia had taken the lead in ASEAN in seeking political accommodation with China and Vietnam. Nevertheless, she was pleased by the willingness of the new rulers in Bangkok to improve border security arrangements[14] and by the readiness of Indonesia to do likewise.[15] She welcomed the bilateral co-operation on security among ASEAN states which the changed situation in Vietnam had helped to bring about, for the internal security of Malaysia had recently shown signs of deterioration.

When the terrorist leader, Chin Peng, took to the jungle in 1960 to rest and recuperate, 500-600 of his followers remained of the 8,000-10,000 at the height of the 1948-60 emergency. In the last three years terrorist incidents have increased, and the number of regular guerrillas (uniformed and armed) runs as high as 2,000 – even higher, according to some private estimates. One reason advanced for the increased activity is the emergence of three rival factions, each competing for prime revolutionary credentials. But more fundamental causes can also be found. Despite the good performance of the Malaysian economy and the strength of its exports of timber, tin, palm oil and rubber, the gap between rich and poor has actually widened since Malaysia, or the Malayan Peninsula as it was then, became independent in 1957.[16] The poorer, rural Malay families have suffered most; the richer Malay families, especially those with access to government, have done best. So the old distinction between Malay and Chinese, which was the basis of Chin Peng's insurgency and the reason for his defeat (for his followers were Chinese and identifiable) is no longer so clear. Malays are joining the guerrillas, making common cause with the dissident Moslem Thais on the Malaysian–Thai border, and the enemy is not now so readily distinguishable. The sensational arrests of influential Malays in and around government for allegedly abetting the Communist cause suggests that the challenge to the present political élite lies not so much in

7

terrorism, which is unpopular with the mass of people and in Malaysia's relatively sheltered position would have difficulty, in the absence of a colonial overlord, in becoming a real threat to the state, but in radical Malay reaction to the affluence and corruption of Malay political hegemony.

The constituents of instability in Malaysia include, therefore, the old-style guerrillas, who are disconcerting in their ability to surface unexpectedly all over the country, Malay radicalism, which demonstrated its frustration and strength in the Baling riots of 1974, and political rivalry within the ruling United Malay National Organization (UMNO). Tunku Abdul Rahman (Prime Minister, 1957-70), who was a father figure, kept Malaya and (after 1963) Malaysia benevolently tied to the West, controlling politics through a three-fold alliance of UMNO, the Malayan Chinese Association (MCA) and the Malayan Indian Congress (MIC). The alliance has now been replaced by the National Front, with a more fragmented Chinese component and more effective Malay dominance, which was the instrument of government during Tunku Abdul Razak's administration (1970-76). While the problem of Malay unrest began to show during Razak's prime ministership, he maintained his leadership by a series of initiatives, including a plan to neutralize South-east Asia and establish diplomatic relations with China. Razak's successor, Datuk Hussein Onn, seized the nettle of corruption among Malay political leaders and acted vigorously, but his actions have stirred up rivalries and strong feelings within UMNO, involving Moslem politics, second-generation leadership and ideological issues in a more open and active way than ever before in Malaysia since independence.

It is probable that the political system will stand the strain and that the Malaysian economy is strong enough to continue to provide the country with a base for development. The current five-year plan provides evidence that the government is aware of the need for rural development, and – as most Malays live in rural areas, which the Chinese still avoid whenever possible – this will have some political effect. Political instability remains, however, and the problem of Moslem politics is that it is not easy to contain within national borders. Singapore,

predominantly Chinese, is sensitive to any revival of Islam in South-east Asia, and Indonesia, only nominally Moslem and politically conservative, also watches radical Malay politics closely.

Indonesia

In Indonesia the emergence of Vietnam as a unified, Communist state and a regional power was an event of great importance, for Vietnam is the only nation capable of contesting Indonesia's right to be thought first among equals in the region. Indonesia has always been tantalized by the belief that, if the external powers could be excluded, she would be accepted as the predominant regional power because of her size, her population, her resources and her strategic position. Sukarno's instinct to throw out Britain and the United States was sound in that respect. His problem was that he could not arouse sufficient support from his neighbours and was forced to invite in other external powers, the Soviet Union and then China, to help: his anti-Communist army leadership did not feel inclined to expend its energy confronting external enemies whose presence it half-condoned, while the enemy within, the Indonesian Communist Party, was encouraged.

Lately Indonesia has been mollified, if not entirely reassured, by the prospect of a more restrained China and detente between the United States and the Soviet Union.[17] She has adopted a low posture in defence and foreign policy. Now she must take account of Vietnam – Communist, armed to the teeth and apparently determined to have a role in the region – and she cannot be sure, looking at the state of great-power relations, if Vietnam might act without restraint, or as the proxy of one Communist power, or might even, perhaps, be competitively propelled by both.

Moreover, Vietnam is emerging as a military power at a time when Indonesia's own military capability is low. One of the characteristics of the Suharto regime, for which it has not been given enough credit by its critics, is that it has been rigorous in using precious foreign exchange for economic development rather than for the purchase of arms. It adopted the philosophy that development was security, which was unusual ten years ago for a military regime, and attested to the common sense of Suharto and some of the military leaders around him and, perhaps especially, to the role of the Western-trained civilian technocrats, whose philosophy it was and is. The strength of the Indonesian army remains about 200,000, which is only slightly in excess of Thailand's, and the air and naval equipment which the Soviet Union sold to Indonesia in the early 1960s has been allowed to run down without significant replacement. The initial response in Djakarta to the rush of events in Vietnam in 1975 was that defence expenditure should be sharply and immediately increased, but 1975 was also a time of financial difficulty in Indonesia, following the discovery that Pertamina, the state oil company, had accumulated massive and urgent debts. The result was a request to the United States for $42 million of arms assistance, mainly for improved surveillance and light air and naval reaction forces, and a joint project with Malaysia for the manufacture of small arms.

Indonesia's request to the United States for more sophisticated surveillance equipment draws attention to the problem of refugees from Indo-China, which is concerning all countries in the region. A unique feature of the refugee flow are the so-called 'boat refugees', who have been leaving Vietnam in small boats and drifting down through the archipelago. According to the United Nations High Commissioner for Refugees, by the end of January 1977 about 2,500 of these had been accounted for, distributed throughout the archipelago. Most have settled in Thailand, but Malaysia and Indonesia have received a large proportion.[18] Indonesian officials are especially concerned about these refugees who may, they reasonably argue, contain people who are, from their point of view, a security risk. In any case, the movement of these 'boat refugees' throughout the waters of the archipelago has indicated the inadequacy of Indonesia's maritime security, and has given stimulus to the debate already taking place in Indonesia, and which is likely to intensify, about the adequacy of her defence. In 1975 Timor raised doubts about Indonesia's military capability. Faced with the prospect that the left-wing group Fretilin had won power, Djakarta decided to move troops into Timor to prevent the formation of an enclave which might look for support outside the region. The international controversy over Indonesia's suppression of Fretilin, and particularly the clumsy manner of the operation, raised questions in Djakarta about whether Indonesia was capable of mounting and sustaining such an expeditionary force. In a country as dispersed as Indonesia the present lack of a naval and air capability to maintain law and order, let alone engage an aggressor, is causing concern.

This concern about defence is linked with anxiety about the economy. Despite an almost doctrinaire commitment to development in the last ten years, and despite some achievements, Indonesia is today, like many Third World countries, still struggling to make a dent in the massive problems of poverty, landlessness and population growth. Indonesia's credit remains good, although the Pertamina crash sent tremors of misgiving throughout the world of international finance. The concern about the economy centres on whether the government can hold to its present development strategy, which is so unambiguously directed towards laying down the infrastructure of a modern state integrated with the international capitalist system, and involves calling on Western technology, money and skills for the construction of and rehabilitation of roads, railways and harbours and the building of industrial estates and plants. Even with projected growth rates, which may be optimistic, both overt and disguised unemployment will continue to rise; landlessness, especially in Java, will increase, and a high inflation rate will persist. There is now more emphasis on rural development and the generation of employment, but the capital-intensive projects undertaken in the heyday of the oil boom cannot be abandoned half-way and will continue to be a drain on resources.

The pattern of economic inequality in the midst of apparent growth in Indonesia is seen in Thailand and Malaysia as well. The poorest are relatively, and sometimes absolutely, poorer.[19] In the view of some austere Western economists, developing countries have to choose between the demands of social justice and economic development, but, for a government, making that choice is not easy. In the case of Indonesia, where the commitment to development has been so vigorous, there is now a reaction, not yet easy to perceive but clear enough to anyone discussing these matters in Djakarta, against a continued low political profile and in favour of a more assertive and nationalist leadership. The concentration on development, it is said by some, has weakened the armed forces. It has, say others, made Indonesia too dependent on advanced Western nations. Others are critical of the corruption and affluence which development has brought to the big cities. Some, especially serious Moslems, are critical of the moral tone of government. Others say that the spirit of Indonesian nationalism has been lost and that it is difficult to convince the youth of the importance of the tasks of building a nation when, after years of devotion to the economy, Indonesians are still among the world's poorest people and, *per capita,* noticeably poorer than their smaller ASEAN colleagues, the Philippines, Singapore, Malaysia and Thailand. They say that Indonesians are not 'economic animals' and, without glamourizing Sukarno, are starting to look back to the spirit of his times with nostalgia.

While Suharto, a modest, pragmatic leader and an institutionalist, remains in power, a return to Sukarnoism is improbable and any renewed sense of Indonesian nationalism is more likely to show itself in tougher bargaining on economic issues and a strengthening of the armed forces, rather than in the manipulation of international politics and the glorification of Indonesian expansion. Nevertheless, even a restrained return to nationalism, accompanied by a concern for the security of the region, would place Indonesia on a course of greater activity, and perhaps leadership in regional affairs, than has been the case since 1965. It is hard to believe that Indonesia will not now take a keen interest in the future of Thailand, especially as the military leaders in Djakarta believe that they have shown themselves to be successful, since independence, in controlling Communism. Djakarta's interest in Malaysia's future is self-evident and vital.

Singapore and the Philippines
Events in Vietnam have had a less direct effect on the other ASEAN states, Singapore and the Philippines. Singapore's fortunes rise and fall with the tide of international commerce. The strong leadership of Lee Kuan Yew, confirmed again in elections in 1976, and the high quality of the administration have reduced the problems of internal security in Singapore.[20] Singapore's main security concern is the internal condition of Malaysia, even more than Indonesia, which was at one time her pre-occupation.[21] Her position is no longer strategically central, as it was when Britain used her as the pivot of naval dominance in South-east Asia, although Singapore has something to contribute in the form of ideas and resolution to her more exposed ASEAN colleagues.

The Philippines, on the other hand, has a history of dissidence and rebellion. Her current pre-occupation is a substantial insurgency in the southern island of Mindanao,[22] where a Moslem rebel group, the Moro National Liberation Front, are claiming autonomy. Despite high-level attention (not only from President Marcos but also from Libya) negotiations have been difficult. However, the Philippines is physically detached from the mainland of South-east Asia and, as has already been noted, is the only member of ASEAN with a bilateral security treaty with the United States. Her importance lies mainly in that relationship with the United States, as the treaty represents a commitment by the United States which, according to the Guam Doctrine, will be honoured. In addition, the terms Manila negotiates with Washington for continued American use of the several bases on Philippine territory, especially Subic Bay naval base and Clark Field air base, will be a test of at least three important elements in any consideration of future forms of security for South-east Asia: the American strategic profile in the Asia–Pacific region; the attitude of Vietnam to the continuance of American bases in South-east Asia, and, not least, Manila's own desire to be seen moving towards a posture of non-alignment or of equidistance in its relations with the major powers.

IV. THE INDO-CHINA STATES

The Communist states of Indo-China are neither united in outlook nor devoid of problems, and it should not be expected that they will easily join together, economically, politically or militarily. Already interesting differences between Vietnam and Cambodia are noticeable. While Hanoi leans towards the Soviet Union, tending to take Moscow's view on world issues, Cambodia has leaned towards Peking. The harshness of social change since the Khmer Rouge took over in April 1975 has provoked particularly bitter criticism in the West, and Cambodia has remained more closed to the outside world than either Laos or Vietnam.

Vietnam: Domestic and Foreign Policy

The penetration of Laos by Vietnam has already been noted. Cambodia's anxiety to avoid Vietnamese penetration is long-standing, illustrated during the Vietnam War by Sihanouk's studied neutrality on the issue of sanctuary, which so annoyed Washington. Vietnam, for her part, has two well-established strategic principles. She is suspicious of China because of their common border, the size of China and a history of conflict. The principle of balance applies here, as it applies to all states confronted with large neighbours who wish to avoid submergence: Vietnam seems to be following the example of Yugoslavia rather than that of Albania – no strident support for the Soviet Union against China (to reverse Albania's early position), but a definite leaning towards the Soviet Union and Eastern Europe, although it would require a shift to urgency or danger for Vietnam to offer the Soviet Union a military presence, perhaps in the form of a naval base. The second of Vietnam's strategic principles is that a dominant position in Laos is necessary for her own security. She will be particularly sensitive to this principle if Cambodia develops close relations with China. China has roads into Laos, extending to the Thai border. The presence of Vietnamese troops in Laos can be related not only to developments in relations between Laos and Thailand, and to internal problems in Laos, but also to the need to show China that Laos is Vietnam's domain.

Vietnam has often been supposed to have hegemonic aims in Indo-China. She is seen by some as the Prussia or Assyria of South-east Asia, who will unify the Indo-China states under her own powerful leadership. This is possible, but it is too early yet to be sure that the new Vietnam will take that course. For one thing, we do not know what view would be formed by the Soviet Union and China of such a development. For another, Vietnam has shown that, whatever her long-term intentions, her short-term pre-occupation is her own economy. So, whatever aspirations may be disguised or suppressed in Hanoi, there is at present a determination not to export revolution or Vietnamese military authority while the work of reconstruction is undertaken. Laos is of no value to Vietnam economically. If peace can be maintained in the region, the preoccupation with national security in Laos will diminish significantly.

These constraints on Vietnam are especially strong because of the economic strategy she has adopted, involving an urgent search for foreign capital. Vietnam surprised the outside world with her early application to join the International Monetary Fund (IMF) and Asian Development Bank, and with the vigour with which she has pursued foreign investment. On a visit to Sweden in February 1977, the Deputy Minister for Foreign Affairs, Nguyen Co Thach, was reported as saying: 'We welcome all foreign investors; we discriminate against nobody; even American enterprises would be welcome to invest in my country.'[23] The problem, the Minister said, was long-term, low-interest credit. According to a Yugoslav report, the Japanese Nomura Institute had estimated that $15,000 million was needed for the reconstruction of Vietnam. An agreement had already been signed with the Soviet Union for aid to the value of $500 million, and the total of aid from the Socialist bloc was expected to be $3,000 million. Sweden, France and Japan had concluded agreements on 'economic co-operation and aid' worth $400 million. The report said that Vietnam also wanted 'co-operation' with Japanese banks.[24] A newspaper report early in 1977, based on Washington sources, suggested that Hanoi had already been promised $6,000 million in aid.[25] In a review of the visit to India in February 1977 by Mr Phan Hien, described as special envoy of the Prime Minister, a commentator on All-India Radio said: 'It has come as a surprise to some that the Vietnamese envoy did no quibbling about the terms and outlook for investment from India. Besides the state level assistance which India might render to Vietnam, he spelt out terms for joint endeavour, both from the public sector in India and the private sector.'[26] In her foreign policy Vietnam has presented herself as actively interested in maintaining normal and peaceful relations with all countries, including the industrial democracies and, especially, her neighbours in South-east Asia. She joined the non-aligned movement and quickly established diplomatic relations with all her non-Communist Asian neighbours, despite her criticism of the ASEAN group at the non-aligned summit meeting in Colombo in August 1976.

By 1977, after the Thailand border incidents and general exchanges of recrimination with Bangkok, a harder tone, which had been glimpsed at the non-aligned summit meeting, began to reappear. Criticisms were made in Hanoi that in 1976 diplomatic and trade relations had expanded too fast.[27] The United States was attacked for trying to use Thailand as a military bridgehead to return to South-east Asia and was referred to as 'the most powerful and cruellest of imperialists', making clearly the point that the Chinese view of a more benign United States was not shared.[28] Vietnam supported the Soviet point of view on Eastern Europe, as, for example, on the charter of the 77 Group in Czechoslovakia.[29] She accused President Carter of using beautiful words like 'freedom' and 'dignity', and asked about the millions of unemployed and the Blacks in the United States, the American youths who were encouraged to massacre the Vietnamese people, the Palestinians, Communists machine-gunned in Spain, the Rosenbergs, the Pinochet massacre of Chilean patriots, the present repression of the Thai people. The list was long and the tone emotional. The general view taken was that Western capitalism was in crisis.

Hanoi's cohesive leadership, no doubt, includes its hawks and doves, and the anti-American tone of early 1977 could have been a defensive response to the fact that developments in Thailand had revived rumours of a return of American influence to Bangkok at the time that the Hanoi leaders were negotiating with the United States for a visit by President Carter's special commission under Leonard Woodcock. Gradually, relations between Vietnam and the United States progressed during 1977, leading to a decision by Washington not to oppose Vietnam's admission to the United Nations.

Reconstruction: The Problems facing Vietnam

A strand in Vietnam's development since 1975 has been the supremacy of the northern part over the southern. The government of unified Vietnam is essentially the former government of North Vietnam. The Provisional Revolutionary Government of the Republic of South Vietnam, created in 1969 and recognized by some states in 1975 after the fall of the Thieu government, was given short shrift in the swift reunification of the country which took place by June 1976. Hanoi is the capital; Saigon is now Ho Chi Minh City.[30] The flag and anthem remain those of former North Vietnam. The predicted bloodbath did not ensue, but the effects of reunification have nevertheless been painful.[31]

Different opinions are held about the reason for the dominance of the north over the south,[32] with the emphasis on economic and political, rather than ideological or security factors. One major problem with which the Vietnamese leaders had to deal was inflation and rising unemployment in the south. To move people from Saigon to the 'new economic zones' in uncleared land in the countryside required strong authority, as the typical resident of former Saigon has no hankering for a plot of land in the wilderness. Control of commodities in short supply was also essential. But it would be surprising if the chief reason for northern predominance were not the simple political fact that the war for national liberation had been fought by Hanoi for thirty years, only latterly with some assistance from sympathizers in the south. The nature of South Vietnamese society had become so different from that of the North during those thirty years, and the political and administrative talent available in the 'national democratic' South so unprepared for the task of reconstruction ahead, that swift reunification and 'socialism' provided the safest course. What we still have to await is the nature of the 'socialism'. It is evidently different from both the Soviet and the Chinese varieties, in that it seems to be seeking a more balanced development of heavy and light industry and agriculture than was the case in either the Soviet or Chinese early experience, and an early opening to the Western financial world. The concentration of industry in the north and a strong base for agriculture in the south provides Vietnam with a potentially strong economy, but at this stage the economy is suffering from low productivity, antiquated plant and inadequate infrastructure.[33] Where its dependencies will lie in the future will depend on the success of Vietnam's international search for capital.

One problem Vietnam faces is that she has arrived late on the development scene, when capital is short and enthusiasm low. If capital is not available, there may be no substitute for the long, slow haul of 'self-reliance' – the 'Vietnamese way of socialism' – and while there is no doubt that Vietnam is quite capable of undertaking it if she has to, the choice would (in turn) affect Hanoi's foreign relations. An open, 'international' policy would forge links with the Western industrial world as well as with the ASEAN group. If Vietnam turns inward, she will turn increasingly to the Soviet Union and will probably also look more to her relations with her Communist neighbours, Laos and Cambodia, which may perhaps not be to their advantage.

Cambodia

Cambodia, renamed Democratic Kampuchea, became a country of mystery after the fall of Phnom Penh to the Khmer Rouge in April 1975. Mystery surrounded the top leadership. The fate of Prince Sihanouk was uncertain. Even the name of the organization providing the political leadership was disputed.[34] A vast social reconstruction now appears to be taking place: the monarchy has been abolished, Buddhism is no longer the state religion, and there have been well-informed reports that the educated middle class has been virtually eliminated, shops abolished and that a self-reliant agrarian economy, based on communes, is to become the basis of Cambodian society. Although the figures are difficult to verify, it appears that hundreds of thousands of Cambodians have died in this transformation since the war ended.[35] In these circumstances a question-mark hangs over Cambodia's future. It is likely, at least, to be a long time before Cambodia is active in regional affairs. In foreign policy she has remained within the non-aligned movement, although she has sided, on issues, with China, her main trading partner and only major supplier of economic aid. Cambodia instituted relations with Albania, Romania and Yugoslavia, but not with the Soviet Union or other Eastern European states. Relations with Vietnam have been cool. Indeed, by contrast – until the coup in Thailand in October 1976 – relations with Bangkok were developing well. Unlike Hanoi, Phnom Penh has not called for American assistance to rebuild the country.[36] While there were frequent exchanges of visits with a range of countries, by the end of 1976 only nine countries had permanent representatives in Phnom Penh – Albania, China, Cuba, Egypt, Laos, North Korea, Romania, Vietnam and Yugoslavia. Cambodia's main security concern would continue to be her age-old problem of relations with her neighbours, Vietnam and Thailand, both larger and more adventurous than herself. To deal with this, she will want to maintain good relations with Laos and to develop her links with Peking.[37]

Laos

Laos, landlocked and poor, has always been dependent on outside support for her economic survival.[38] The movement of Vietnamese troops in and out of Laos is stark evidence of this dependence but, in addition, Soviet and Vietnamese aid has been accepted, while links with Western countries have been cut. The exodus of officials, businessmen and skilled personnel during 1976 reflected economic set-backs and political unrest. However, Laos, unlike Cambodia, received the Woodcock mission and allowed the United States to maintain a care-taker embassy in Vientiane. Rather than turn to China, with which she shares a border, Laos seemed to want to look again to the United States to preserve a balance in her necessarily dependent relations with Hanoi and Moscow.

V. THE EXTERNAL POWERS

A Balance of Power in South-East Asia?

When the United States withdrew from Vietnam and began to disengage from South-east Asia, the implications of this action were not entirely clear. Where there new objectives? What would be the strategic profile of the United States in the Asia–Pacific region?

The United States abandoned a two-and-a-half-war strategy for a one-and-a-half-war strategy; that is, she would maintain forces to meet a major attack in Europe or in Asia but not, as before, in both at the same time, while retaining the 'half' for a contingency elsewhere. Various pronouncements, beginning with the Guam Doctrine in 1969, and coupled with President Nixon's dramatic visit to China in 1972, confirmed the impression that the changes required by the new doctrine would be felt almost entirely in Asia. However, this assumption was partly the product of conflicting statements at a high level in Washington, followed by fearful responses in many Asian countries, and was not justified by what actually occurred in American military planning. The intention of the Guam Doctrine and its progeny may have been, as suggested, to make a continued American presence in the Asia–Pacific region palatable to American public opinion and especially to Congress.[39] The test will now come with decisions to be taken by the Carter Administration on the kind of military presence to maintain in Korea in order to bolster the security treaty with Seoul, on the status of the United States' relationship with Taiwan and on the arrangements made with the Philippines over the bases at Subic Bay and Clark Field.

Washington's conception of a power balance, as it has affected Asia, has been confined so far to keeping both the Soviet Union and China off balance. By establishing contact with China, the United States has had the advantage of communication with both Moscow and Peking, who lack useful communication with each other. The United States has had no control over relations between the two Communist rivals, but she has had the capacity to manipulate and to be suggestive. This off-balance relationship has excluded Japan, however, who has sought to establish her own relations with the Soviet Union and China, while remaining an ally of

the United States. Neither Moscow nor Peking has wished to see sudden changes of incalculable consequence to their own tense relationship.

What we have been observing since 1969 in Asia is, therefore, not really a balance of power, but a disinclination by the four states to make major moves which would affect the present stand-off. This disinclination is not yet the result of the recognition of any preferred state of relationships, such as the inherent virtue of a balance, but of a combination of factors, partly internal, such as China's leadership crisis and the long wait in the United States for an elected president who can hope to carry the country with him in foreign policy, and partly a reflection of a change in priorities in world politics, since economic rather than military considerations have played a more important part in great-power calculations in the first half of the 1970s.

Relations between the Soviet Union and China do not give an impression of stability. Indeed the Soviet Union, having been disadvantaged by the improvement in United States–China relations, and being herself encumbered with a two-war, if not a two-and-a-half-war strategy, would see her relations in Asia as closely connected with, if not, indeed, even a function of, her relations in Europe, in the same way as the North Atlantic Treaty Organization (NATO) powers would see the balance of military power in Europe as sustained by the assumption of continuing hostility between China and the Soviet Union and the necessary commitment of a certain level of Soviet forces to the China border. The Soviet Union would, no doubt, like to improve her relations with China and would certainly fear the prospect of some kind of arrangement or understanding in security between the United States and China, especially if Japan were involved. She would then be hemmed in on both sides by the United States and her allies. Japan, although clear at this stage that she wishes to remain an ally of the United States, would not want the conflict between China and the Soviet Union to intensify so that fruitful relations with one excluded fruitful relations with the other. This has already been shown by Japan's reluctance to sign the 'anti-hegemony' clause, directed against the Soviet

Union, in her peace treaty with China. Japan's position is strengthened by rivalry between China and the Soviet Union which, however, stops short of conflict. Japan can hope to gain the maximum terms from each in order to prevent either from feeling that she is forming a special relationship with the other. But were the Sino-Soviet split to become intense and spill over into military conflict, Japan would face the worst possible outcome, which is that she would be drawn into the conflict.

Relations between the external powers in South-east Asia will be affected by their relations in Asia generally, and in particular in north Asia, but it need not be assumed they will be determined by their relationship outside the region. It may be useful, therefore, to look at their interests in South-east Asia, to the extent that they can be isolated.

The United States
American interests in South-east Asia were so inflated during the Vietnam War that it is still difficult not to protest that they are much less substantial than they have been made out. In summary, however, they are still significant. In all ASEAN states the United States is a major investor and trader and maintains a strong resident American business community. She gives military aid to Thailand, Malaysia, Indonesia and the Philippines. In the case of the Philippines, she has, in addition, a mutual security treaty and bases which are related to her own security interests. In an early indication of the attitude of the Carter Administration to these interests, an official described the treaty with the Philippines, and American use of the bases, as serving 'important US national interests today, just as they did during World War II and during the war in Vietnam. They contribute significantly to the maintenance of stability in South-east Asia and to our ability to keep vital sea lanes open in the event of hostilities'.[40]

The interest of the United States in 'stability' is partly her own, in that, as a major investor, she wishes to see the maintenance of regimes in South-east Asia somewhat like those at present in control of the ASEAN states, as these are broadly sympathetic to capitalist investment. It reflects also the wishes of Japan and Australia, with whom the United States has substantial

security relationships. Differences could arise between these three on the meaning of 'stability', but at the moment there is broad agreement that it is in their interests for the current pattern of pro-Western politics in ASEAN to continue. The interest in 'vital sea lanes' is also shared by Japan and Australia, both of whom wish to see South-east Asia maintained as a transit and trans-shipment centre, but the United States has a special interest, as a global military power, in being able to move her warships, including submarines, between the Pacific and Indian Oceans through South-east Asia, which means, in effect, through the several straits which Indonesia partially or wholly controls. The Carter Administration has drawn attention to another concern, more difficult to define and sometimes apparently in conflict with her interest in stability: the maintenance of certain institutions which strengthen the growth of democracy and democratic practices in South-east Asia. The situation is not promising for democracy, if by democracy is meant the free election of genuinely alternative governments from time to time. But there is room for optimism if one expects something less, yet still, in human terms, positive – a genuine intention to improve living standards, absence of official terror and brutality, relatively open education with a concern for scholarship, freedom of citizens to travel abroad and receive information from abroad, non-government-sponsored newspapers and other sources of information and authority in the community. A society which allows its citizens these kinds of freedoms is likely to turn more to the United States and the industrial democracies than to the Soviet Union, the People's Republic of China or the Socialist Republic of Vietnam.

Japan
Japan's interests in South-east Asia are somewhat similar to those of the United States, but more intensely economic. Japan has now outpaced the United States as the major trader and investor of South-east Asia.[41] Since her late entry into the foreign capital market (about 1970), Japan has made an impression on South-east Asia dramatic enough to arouse resentment, although in the famous case of the riots in Djakarta in 1974, associated with Mr Tanaka's visit, it is not altogether clear to what

15

extent the riots were directed against the Japanese rather than the Suharto government for failures of the nationalist spirit, including submission to Japan. Japan has no military interest in transit, although she has a major commercial interest in South-east Asia as an accessible waterway. Her security interests are not comparable with those in north Asia and she has been reluctant to take a more active political role in the region. She has an interest in the commercial freedoms of democracy, but tends not to take stands on issues of human rights.

Japan's concern that South-east Asia should remain open to foreign investment is much greater than the United States', and the cases of Thailand and Indonesia are especially important. If these countries were evidently likely to come under the control of either Communist or intensely nationalist governments which could threaten Japanese investment, Japan might be forced to play a political part in trying to prevent this. She would be unlikely to act quickly; it is clear that Japan is able to deal effectively with a wide range of governments and systems. Yet it is also true that of all the major powers Japan is the most engaged in South-east Asia and at the same time the most insecure. Without a military capability abroad, Japan feels uncertain about the security of her economic investments in an area like South-east Asia, where she is too visible and has too dramatic a history to be entirely politically detached, as she is in Latin America or the Middle East. Her unpopularity in South-east Asia is well known. To keep the area economically manageable she feels the need for a stabilizing influence, which she sees at the moment as the function of the United States, with support from Australia. This psychological dependence on the United States makes the impact of Japan's notable economic strengths in South-east Asia unpredictable, and gives her influence in the region an uncertain, and even brittle, appearance.[42]

China

Japan's main rival in South-east Asia is China, because both are Asian and both feel that, if spheres of influence are being handed around, South-east Asia should be theirs. While Japan's influence is economic and entrepreneurial, China's is cultural and perhaps political. Japan was the effective agent of anti-colonialism in South-east Asia in World War II and was also, incidentally, an agent of destruction of the Kuomintang in China, which must cause her some thought today. In South-east Asia now, however, she is a *status quo* power, whereas China is caught between two strengths – her influence within the Chinese communities and revolutionary groups in South-east Asia, and her strategic interest in stability, provided by the present governments of the region. China is a Communist state with revolutionary objectives, and it is no credit to China and the immense experiment carried out there in the name of Communism to suppose that she will lose all enthusiasm for social and political change in South-east Asia simply to keep the Soviet Union out. China could have a powerful influence on the politics of South-east Asia, if she chose to support dissident movements more vigorously and were to use her power within the Chinese communities to agitate for revolutionary change. Yet this potential strength is also a weakness. Owing to its proximity, its size, its cultural influence and its traditional view of South-east Asia as an area of the world naturally disposed to pay tribute to China, Peking is watched with suspicion in the region. It has moved lately with caution, being as reassuring as possible to the national leaders and keeping a low profile on local issues. Its comments on the effects of the military coup in Bangkok, even when Thailand and Cambodia, its prodigy, were in conflict, were modest. It maintains good relations with Hanoi, patiently riding out Moscow's predominance. In particular, Peking has been careful not to push the United States too hard or too far. At the same time it maintains support for the Thai Communist Party, the Burma Communist Party, the Malayan (*sic*) Communist Party and the Indonesian Communist Party.

The question of stability in South-east Asia remains a dilemma for China, especially as her economic influence in the region is not marked.[43] She could face a particularly difficult test of policy in Thailand, where the prospect of serious Communist insurgency is greatest. While the United States and Japan have economic difficulties with Asian nationalism, China has political difficulties, for the political nationalists in South-east Asia tend to be anti-Chinese.[44]

So while Peking may hope that its claim on some kind of ascendancy in South-east Asia will gradually become more acceptable, the prospect at present does not look bright, unless there is substantial economic and social change. The nationalist leaders of South-east Asia appreciate that China is not at present opposing an American military presence in or near the region because Peking does not want Moscow to be given the opportunity to move in, but they also appreciate, on their own behalf, that an American presence gives them a useful counter to China as well as to the Soviet Union. The sustained belief of Peking and its supporters that China has a special claim on South-east Asia, different in kind from the claims made by the Soviet Union, the United States or Japan, is not widely shared in the region itself.

The Soviet Union

The Soviet Union has not had the same difficulties with Asian nationalism since the 1940s and 1950s, when she tried to topple the new nationalist leaders without success. She has developed policies to deal with Asian nationalism and, in the case of Vietnam, India and, to a lesser extent, Indonesia, Thailand and Malaysia, has had some success. She plays upon anti-Chinese sentiment. However, she is also a rival of the United States.

Soviet economic and military aid has been at times substantial, to Indonesia (until 1965), for example, and Vietnam. But Soviet trade with the region is small.[45] Only with Malaysia, whose exports of rubber to the Soviet Union are increasing, does it amount to more than 3 per cent of the country's total exports. The Soviet Union's main activity in South-east Asia is diplomatic and political. Through cultural exchanges, official visits and the growth of her merchant ship and commercial aircraft fleets, as well as her navy, she has given an impression of activity on the increase, although the activity is still small. The fact that the Soviet Union is a super-power, with a military capability about that of the United States, attracts respect and attention. There is a tendency to confer on the Soviet presence in South-east Asia a status comparable to that which it has in Europe and in the nuclear equation with the United States. This has happened especially in respect of the small naval presence the Soviet Union maintains

in the Indian Ocean; Moscow has reaped political benefits from the attention lavished on its maritime presence.

In South-east Asia, the Soviet Union has shown herself particularly interested in Indonesia (1959-65) and in Indo-China, especially Vietnam, since the 1954 Geneva Conference. She was co-chairman with Britain of the 1962 Geneva Agreement to neutralize Laos and has always taken an active role in the politics of Indo-China. Should the United States or China make a bad mistake in South-east Asia, or should a revolutionary movement appear likely to gain success, Soviet policy is opportunistic enough and sufficiently broad-based to seek to take advantage. But South-east Asia does not seem to be in the forefront of Soviet thinking, as north and south Asia, the Middle East and Africa are. Mr Brezhnev's proposal for a collective security system for Asia was an attempt at grand diplomacy, aimed primarily, one supposes, at the remnants of regional groupings described earlier in this paper, left behind in the wake of the American withdrawal from Vietnam and the decision to dissolve SEATO. Launched in 1969, it has had a marked lack of success and although it remains an article of faith with Soviet official spokesmen, the proposition has become something of a ritual. Nothing has been done to sharpen its vague outlines, which both confuse and tantalize, and it seems to indicate a rather haphazard interest in current developments in South-east Asia.

In one matter the Soviet Union and the United States have similar interests: neither wants nationalism to become aggressive in South-east Asia to the extent that access to the waterway is threatened. Even more than the United States, the Soviet Union has a specific interest in moving her ships from the Pacific to the Indian Ocean, as this is the only all-weather route between the east and the west of the country. The United States is provided on both sides with all-weather ports, and ships can go east-about or west-about as they please (assuming the Panama Canal stays open, but even without it the transport problems faced are minor compared with those of the Soviet Union). Soviet interest in maintaining South-east Asia as an area of relative stability and international access is therefore keen, and is another reason for supposing that her policies in the

17

region will tend to continue to be cautious and low-key. The Soviet Union is feared in Europe because she is near at hand and has shown that she is prepared to act brutally to enforce stability in her own interests. Her suppression of dissent and her failure to create an intellectually attractive society make her unpopular in the West. These weaknesses are not so apparent in Asia, especially in South-east Asia, which is distant from her. Soviet influence in the area is probably the lowest among the four external powers, but the Soviet Union has used her modest influence quite successfully to monitor the activities of the United States and China.

The picture of the external powers which emerges is that, while they have different interests in South-east Asia, they are all concerned to preserve some kind of stability in the area, although they would not be able to agree publicly on what that stability means. Each seems constrained at the moment from acting in a way which would upset the others. They do not see South-east Asia as a vantage point from which any of them is likely to want to threaten the others. They all – though this is least certain in the case of China – have an interest in seeing the region of South-east Asia

remain open as an international concourse linking two major oceans and the trade routes between Australia and New Zealand in the south, and China and Japan in the north. In the absence of a more deliberate and settled relationship between the four powers than at present exists, the possibility always remains that they may be drawn into conflicts which arise within the region. An 'interest' is not unchanging, and sometimes long-term objectives have to be abandoned or postponed in order to permit response to short-term predicaments. But there does not seem to be a high probability of conflict at present. The United States would do much to avoid another conflict in South-east Asia; Japan is not in a position to become engaged in one; and the Soviet Union, in contrast to her eagerness in the Middle East and Africa, and reflecting the fact that she now has an opportunity to consolidate her influence in Vietnam, has shown no interest in being drawn. China, facing internal dissension, would seem the most likely to participate, but has been extremely cautious in the past. Facing the Soviet Union in the north, and with unresolved questions such as the future of Taiwan to explore with the United States, China, too, is likely to continue to be patient.

VI. WHAT COULD GO WRONG?

The foregoing description of reactions within the region to developments in Vietnam, and of the current state of relations between the external powers, suggests that South-east Asia can expect a future of uncertainty while the region is divided within itself and the external powers are undecided about their future roles. There are four kinds of security problem:

(1) Political instability and insurgency supported from outside, especially from Peking and Hanoi, are a problem in some ASEAN countries, especially Thailand. While the probability of military intervention from outside these countries is not high, it is not entirely absent. A weakening of government could bring about a loss of physical control so that territory could be occupied and force used by a neighbour at low risk. In the case of Thailand, it is not at all

difficult to foresee a situation developing in the provinces contiguous to Laos and Cambodia which would allow the surreptitious occupation of Thai territory by forces from across the border, including those from Vietnam. Now that political leadership is available to the Thai Communist Party from defecting intellectuals, it may not prove hard to find leaders who could be projected as a national alternative to the government in Bangkok. Thailand would then be faced with the prospect of a civil war more substantial than the insurgencies with which she has been troubled in the last ten years.

Even without outside support, such a civil conflict would be debilitating. If Vietnam provided support, it could prove difficult for the Soviet Union and China not to be supportive also, in the way each assisted Hanoi in the Vietnam War. Neither might be enthusiastic, but neither would wish the other to become associated alone with a revolutionary war in Thailand, especially if there were grounds for believing that it might be successful. China would be particularly anxious not to be isolated, because her influence in Cambodia could be checked if Hanoi, backed by Moscow, established dominance through Laos and northern Thailand. The fighting between Cambodia and Vietnam which broke out in 1977, *inter alia* in the 'Parrot's Beak' – an area of Cambodian territory which Hanoi had used as a sanctuary for its troops during the Vietnam war – is significant in this context. It not only demonstrated that Cambodia might be vulnerable to Vietnamese pressure, but it also highlighted China's difficulties in maintaining her influence over the regime in Phnom Penh.

One possibility for China, in the event of a revolutionary movement in northern Thailand falling under Vietnamese and/or Soviet control, would be to become more active in Burma. China's links with the Burmese Communist Party (BCP) are well established. The formal tie between the BCP and the Shan and Kachen dissident movement in northern Burma[46] underlines the fact that, since coming to power in 1962, General Ne Win has had little success in quelling the many insurgent movements in Burma, of which the BCP is the largest.[47] Chinese assistance to the BCP has been crucial in keeping operations against the Burmese Government at an irritating level.[48] General Ne Win's tactic has been to avoid public comment on the issue, isolate Burma as much as possible from international politics and pursue good state-to-state relations with China.[49]

(2) Communism remains an issue in South-east Asia because of Vietnam and China. The fact that the ASEAN countries are closely linked with the economies of the Western industrial societies, and are non-Communist in outlook, means that a division of the region could occur on ideological lines. A geographical division of the region could produce a form of balance of power, but an ideological confrontation would increase the prospect of a bloody struggle over Thailand and, probably, more rigid and authoritarian government in the ASEAN states. Mr Lee Kuan Yew's crackdown on 'pro-Communist' elements after his successful election of December 1976 is an indication of how

fear of Communism still haunts one of the most effective nationalist leaders the region has known. The crusade against 'pro-Communists' in Malaysia, although more complex than in Singapore's case, again shows how useful the Communist 'threat' is to any leader in South-east Asia. This is not the occasion to reflect on what exactly the Communist threat is. What it is thought to be, or is presented as being, may be more relevant.

(3) There is the possibility, even if at present most unlikely, that the external powers may be tempted to intervene, either directly or through proxies, or may be induced to take up dominant positions in one country or group of countries. In present circumstances this intervention would be more likely to be political and economic rather than military, although if the United States retains use of the Philippine bases, one might suppose that the Soviet Union will continue to look hopefully towards Vietnam, who has a long coastline and some good harbours, for a naval facility of her own. In the economic field the candidate for dominant external power is Japan, who is likely to pay more, rather than less, attention to South-east Asia. On account of her preferred low political profile and lack of military capability, Japan would be ultimately dependent in any conflict on the United States, which makes her position unpredictable and volatile.

The economic dominance of Japan and, to a lesser extent, the United States in South-east Asia inevitably collides with local aspirations for economic and political independence, as it can be viewed as the exploitation of basically poor, rural societies, dependent on commodity prices, by affluent industrial societies who can manipulate the terms of trade. Although the Soviet Union and China can drive a hard bargain and are less forthcoming with economic assistance for development, their centrally planned economies give them a political advantage in their foreign policies in South-east Asia, as in the Third World. Their support for political subversion runs counter to nationalism, whereas the industrial democracies clash with nationalism when their economic influence penetrates too deeply. Both Japan and the United States have shown a readiness to talk with ASEAN as an organization, in order to relate their economic policies to the needs of the

ASEAN region as a whole, which will help prevent concentration by one or both of them on a particular country. However, ASEAN has itself yet to work out a concerted response.

(4) Unresolved disputes, of which there are several, could provoke conflict, in the absence of constraints or consultative forms. Some boundaries in South-east Asia are still unmarked, and while the Law of the Sea remains undetermined there will inevitably be disputes about transit arrangements, fishing rights, smuggling and oil claims. The claim by Manila to territory in eastern Malaysia was gradually resolved by goodwill on both sides and by willing negotiators. But goodwill cannot be assumed in a possible conflict arising out of a complex of claims, for example, to the Spratly Archipelago in the South China Sea, to which China, Taiwan, Vietnam and the Philippines all lay claim, the first three alleging historical rights and the Philippines the rights of occupancy. The Philippines has been granting oil exploration leases since the early 1970s. Philippine troops are garrisoned on five islands, Vietnamese on three and Taiwanese on one.

The sultanate of Brunei, already rich in oil, is another potential trouble spot. Still a British protectorate, with her oil and natural gas resources under the control of the Shell group, she has made no constitutional progress since an abortive rebellion in 1962 led by the Brunei People's Party, which at that time held all the elective seats in the Legislative Assembly. Brunei stayed out of the Malaysian federation in 1963, and the Sultan has looked to the British Gurkha battalion stationed in Brunei for protection both from internal political unrest and pressure from her two big neighbours, Malaysia and Indonesia.

None of these security problems is pressing. One reason is that, unlike other neuralgic global conflict points, there is as yet no concentration of arms in the region, with the exception of Vietnam. However, within a three-to-five year period the elements of conflict in the unrefined mixture of great-power needs and small-power rivalries which characterizes South-east Asia could, if unattended, again become dominant.

VII. NATIONALISM AND INTERNATIONALISM

In the foregoing discussion two substantial themes have been touched upon and now need amplification. One is the importance of nationalism within the region. The other is the requirement by the external powers that South-east Asia should be maintained as a transit and trans-shipment concourse – a waterway. If effective forms of security are to be found, it is evident that they must address these two themes.

Nationalism
Nationalism in South-east Asia remains potent in several ways. First, the territories rather haphazardly bequeathed by the colonial powers have endured surprisingly well. Despite their rivalries, subversions and revolutionary insurgencies, no state created from a colony has yet been submerged within another territory. The formation of the Federation of Malaysias (originally consisting of Malaya, Sabah, Sarawak and Singapore) offended Indonesia and, to some

extent, the Philippines, but it merely brought together in a convenient form British territories which could have had difficulty standing on their own. Singapore, in any case, separated shortly afterwards. Laos is a more difficult case to argue: the country was divided into factional domains, part of it occupied by Vietnamese troops, and compulsorily, although ineffectively, neutralized. Portuguese Timor was absorbed by Indonesia without colonial legitimacy, as it were, and Brunei, still a British protectorate, awaits a future more in keeping with the times. But, generally, the political geography of South-east Asia has been stable, despite its apparent weakness.

So, while it is true that for twenty centuries South-east Asia has been fragmented and diverse, and for a good deal of this period, especially on the mainland, ethnic groups and princely states have expanded and contracted endlessly within each other's territories, since the end of World War II and their occupation for the first time in their history by a single power, Japan, the nation states of South-east Asia have remained territorially firm. Nationalism is, therefore, no longer simply anti-colonialism, or nation-building, but the protection of established territory.

Second, nationalism has been strengthened in recent years by a world-wide emphasis on resources and production, rather than trade. Predictions of a resource-starved world have strengthened the bargaining position in world politics of many Third World countries, in addition to the organization of Petroleum Exporting Countries (OPEC) and its dramatic activities. While resources are not necessarily related to size, the chances are that the larger the country, the better its resource prospects are, so we have seen in South-east Asia that Indonesia and Malaysia are increasing in importance, while Singapore's importance has declined, or, put another way, has been maintained only with great effort. The more significant resources become, the more necessary it is for states to control their hinterlands, and the combination of these economic and security considerations is likely to strengthen nationalism.

Third, the emergence of a unified Vietnam, to which reference has already been made, is likely to stimulate nationalism in South-east Asia. The reasons are not only that the war in Vietnam was long and dramatic, and that the issue of foreign 'domination' has therefore been kept alive, but also that Vietnam is nationalistic, especially in the north where the political core of the country lies. Although Communist, Vietnam's ideology is already showing distinctive traits and her persistent need to balance the influence of China and the Soviet Union will strengthen its distinctiveness. Vietnam is, therefore, likely to give impetus to the view that external powers should never again be allowed to control South-east Asia; she will be looking to balance one external power against another, and especially to see that China does not become dominant in the old Indo-China area. In the long-term she could show some sympathy for Indonesia's view that exclusion has its advantages, but certainly she will be hostile to the idea of a significant external military presence.

Internationalism

So far as the forces of internationalism are concerned, the history of South-east Asia as a waterway is well documented. The early mainland states were essentially riverine, but in the archipelago political evolution followed navigational skill, a development similar to that of then medieval European city state. As the city states and, later, empires flourished, Indian, Arab and Chinese traders arrived. With the rise of the maritime European powers, especially on the Indian sub-continent, the route between the land-breakers in South-east Asia became established, and Malacca, Singapore, Batavia, Manila and Saigon became trading ports and repair centres. Britain made Singapore into her greatest base, intended to protect the sea routes and especially the Malacca Straits. Japan moved her headquarters from Singapore to Saigon during 1942-45, indicating concern with the archipelago's stability. Since World War II, and especially since Japan's dramatic growth as a trading nation, the importance of South-east Asia as a transit area has increased. Singapore has developed her bunkering and trans-shipment facilities. Until recently an Anglo-American military presence effectively straddled the area, providing both protection and economic benefits.

The strategic concept of South-east Asia as a waterway is necessarily difficult to define, but it enshrines the need felt by external countries to use the region for purposes beyond those relevant to the region itself. The need exists today, obviously enough, but not as a right. It has been met in the past by two expedients: those countries who wished to use the area as a waterway were in a position to enforce their need as a right or were able to persuade the resident states that it was in their own interest to allow their waters to be used for the purposes of international trade, commerce and the movement of warships from one ocean to another.

The likelihood that this will continue is strong. South-east Asia is an area bigger than the Mediterranean, with several exit and entry points. It is not a single canal, like Suez or Panama, which can be blocked by the action of a single state or the sinking of a single ship. Moreover, it is itself a source of trade and, unlike Panama or Suez, a trans-shipment centre. Singapore, as an entrepot, has a particular interest in seeing that the world's ships use the South-east Asian route.

However, some refinements of this generally agreeable picture show up possible trouble spots. Of the seven navigable straits in South-east Asia linking the Indian and Pacific Oceans, for example, all are within the archipelago of Indonesia, or are shared by Indonesia with Malaysia.[50] A good deal depends on the goodwill of Indonesia who, with Malaysia, has been more circumspect about the free flow of international traffic than has Singapore. A strongly nationalistic regime in Djakarta, reacting against a failure of the international economy, or engaging in a trial of strength with major states or international companies, might use its control of the waterways to harass or embarrass international users.

At the moment Indonesia is working closely with Singapore and Malaysia, with financial assistance from Japan, to maintain access to and safe navigation of the Malacca Straits,[51] through which, on average, 100 ships pass each day, including tankers carrying the bulk of Japan's oil imports and iron ore from Australia. The three states have been concerned about oil spills, and large tankers have begun using the Lombok and Makassar Straits, which are deeper and wider. It has been reported that a 'super-port' for oil storage and trans-shipment at Palau, in the United States trust territory of Micronesia, is being planned by a consortium of Iranian, Japanese and American oil, banking and industrial interests, with the objective that it should act as an entrepot for the 500,000-ton oil tankers too big for the Malacca Straits.[52] Even with a 12-mile territorial sea limit (which effectively closes the Malacca Straits at the eastern end), the Makassar Straits would be open, in the sense that they would have a high-seas corridor. However, it remains true that a great deal of international shipping would continue to use the Malacca Straits (and the entrepot of Singapore) because they are the most direct route, and neither Indonesia nor Malaysia has been prepared to agree to the description of the Malacca Straits as 'international straits'. The implication of the various and complicated disputes relating to the Law of the Sea need not be reviewed here.[53] It is sufficient to note that Indonesia and Malaysia have different conceptions from those of the Soviet Union, the United States, Japan and Britain of what 'access' and 'transit' mean and that China has tended to support them.[54] Similarly, complex disputes are implied in the notion of 'archipelagic sovereignty', which Indonesia (and the Philippines) support. Indonesia, in particular, feels that her territorial integrity is threatened if waters between the many islands of her archipelago are not subject to Indonesian national sovereignty.

A particular problem arises in the case of the transit of warships, especially submarines. The United States and the Soviet Union take the view that rapid and secret movement of their warships, especially their nuclear-armed submarines, is essential to the reliability of their second-strike nuclear capability and therefore to the balance of nuclear power (on which, they might argue, if pressed, the peace of the world depends). In asserting the law of 'innocent passage', which requires submarines in transit to surface, Malaysia and Indonesia have drawn on two main lines of argument. One is that the nuclear balance between the super-powers cannot be relied on, and innocent passage is required to prevent a war of nerves from taking place in waters in and around South-east Asia. The other is that foreign warships, if undetected, could be used to give support to dissident local groups. Other arguments about pollution and safety have been raised.

However, these ostensibly irreconcilable public positions are not incompatible in practice. It is unlikely that either Indonesia or Malaysia has the means at present to detect the underwater passage of nuclear submarines which, because Malacca is too shallow, use the Lombok and Ombai-Wetar Straits.[55] In addition, the deployment by the United States of the *Trident*-class of submarine-launched ballistic missiles, with ranges of 4,000 – 6,000 nautical miles, will, it is authoritatively claimed, 'virtually eliminate' dependence of American submarines on important international straits within 12-mile territorial limits.[56] In the event of war, of course, legal interpretations of disputed rights are not likely to be decisive.

VIII. TWO OPTIONS

In looking for types of security system for South-east Asia which might both meet the demands of nationalism and promote the continued use of South-east Asia as an international waterway, two possibilities, loosely described below, present themselves.

Regional Groupings: Benefits and Dangers

One would be for the region to divide – some would say naturally – into its mainland and archipelago components, the mainland group comprising the states of former Indo-China, and the archipelago group comprising the ASEAN countries.

ASEAN would become a defence organization capable of protecting its members from regional attack and internal subversion. The five-power arrangements for Malaysia and Singapore would probably remain, as would the United States security treaty with the Philippines. The network of political and military co-operation between the United States, Australia, New Zealand, Indonesia, Malaysia, Singapore and the Philippines, with the likely addition of Papua New Guinea, would persist in the form of military funding, equipment and intelligence sharing, although ASEAN as such would not be supported by treaty arrangements with outsiders. To be effective ASEAN would need to strengthen, in particular, its naval capability. Its existing ground forces would probably be adequate in strength.

The danger in such a division of South-east Asia is, as already noted, that it would be ideological as well as geographical. By dividing on ideological lines, it would invite the external powers in, also on ideological lines. However, against that:

(a) neither Vietnam nor Indonesia would wish to be the proxy of an external power;

(b) The Soviet Union and China would continue to compete in the region, including within the Indo-China bloc, as the United States and Japan would within the ASEAN bloc;

(c) The United States no longer seem interested in having proxies in South-east Asia, which tend to draw her into trouble;

(d) Japan would probably be able to sustain an important economic role in both blocs, as, in a political way, might India;

(e) the archipelago region would continue, under the influence of ASEAN, to provide access to international traffic;

(f) both groups could have relations with the non-aligned movement, although this would require strong leadership by Indonesia on behalf of the ASEAN group and could mean the eventual phasing-out of the five-power arrangements and the American bases in the Philippines.

The practical advantage of the arrangement is that it is already partially in existence and would require the minimum of policy decisions by the external and regional powers. The initiative could come from the ASEAN group, as the result of a decision to adopt a more prominent security function, which would invite Hanoi to strengthen its links with Laos and Cambodia. As the Thai crisis has deepened in 1977, both these developments were foreshadowed. For Cambodia, in particular, who has always suspected Vietnamese intentions, the arrangement would be unpleasant initially, as it would be for some countries in the ASEAN group, particularly, Singapore who would feel uncomfortable in a defence alliance which was inevitably heavily influenced by Indonesia. The same might be said of all such alliances, however – the attitude of France to American leadership of NATO and Romanian attitudes to the Soviet Union are examples.

The arrangement would meet some of the needs of regional security and also the objections of those who feel that the 'region' of south-east Asia is not yet a reality. It would maintain an American, British and Australian influence in the archipelago region, which is where those countries' main interests lie, and would also protect Japan's economic interest in free traffic through the waterway. It would not commend itself to the Soviet Union and China so readily, although it would be plain that the defence arrangements of ASEAN were not of a stature to threaten them. However, the Soviet Union would be disturbed about the possibility that Indonesia would be able to prevent the movement of her warships to the Indian Ocean (although that possibility exists now). China would be concerned that the Soviet Union might respond by trying to establish a substantial military presence in Vietnam, although Vietnam would probably resist such overtures. If she did respond favourably to the Soviet Union, China might look to her own relations with Burma, with Thailand or even, of course, with the Soviet Union.

Yet even when the disadvantages are discounted and the advantages stressed, the formation of opposing military groupings in South-east Asia carries the depressing possibility, indeed likelihood, of a regional arms race. It is conceivable that the four powers, the United States, the Soviet Union, China and Japan, could reach agreement on limiting the flow of arms, but there are other arms suppliers, and the history of arms-control measures suggests that there is an inner dynamic about competition in arms which, once started, is extremely difficult to stop. The great-power stand-off is neither sufficiently secure nor adequately institutionalized for the prospects of an arms-control arrangement of this kind to be rated particularly highly.

If it could be assumed that the two regional groups would be sensible in not deflecting resources from economic development, and in not exciting each other unduly, the prognosis would not be alarming, but if such an assumption could be made in the first place, there would be no reason for the groupings to emerge. It is more likely that the ASEAN states, determined to catch up with Vietnam, would be tempted to purchase sophisticated equipment, and Vietnam, convinced that ASEAN was an instrument for the return of American imperialism, would react.

In any case, the practical difficulty of Thailand remains. Thailand's security weaknesses would be inherited by ASEAN, and while there is a view in some circles that Thailand could be made the forge to turn ASEAN's ploughshares into swords, it is not a dominant view. If military security is the test, a lot of blood will flow down the Mekong before Thailand's position is stable. Perhaps, realizing this, Thailand will begin to see herself again in her traditional role of buffer state. As a member of ASEAN, Thailand's influence would then act as a brake on the development of a military bloc.

Regional Neutrality

The second option, which holds out more hope for the exploration of the informal detente existing at present in South-east Asia, is regional neutrality. This has been most precisely developed in the Malaysian proposal for a zone of peace, friendship and neutrality (ZOPFAN), which has been adopted in principle by the ASEAN states, but the idea of South-east Asia as a neutral zone has been explored more thoroughly.[57]

There is a substantial literature on the differences between 'neutralism', 'neutrality', 'non-alignment' and 'neutralization', which need not stand in the way of a discussion about the practical strengths and weaknesses of the Malaysian proposal, which is a useful model.[58] It envisages increasing consultations and cooperation among the South-east Asian countries themselves and 'recognition of, and respect for, South-east Asia as a zone of peace, freedom and neutrality, free from any form or manner of interference by outside Powers'.[59] The proposal has itself evolved, and there have been different, even opposing, responses to it from within the region. It was initially believed to be, in essence, an offer made to China that she should stay out of Malaysia's affairs, indeed the region's affairs, in return for a withdrawal of American military power. Indonesia was sympathetic, although not towards the idea of being compulsorily 'neutralized' by the great powers (like Austria). Singapore was sceptical, pointing to the example of Laos; she held to the view that the best guarantee of security for ASEAN was an American presence because she doubted whether China or the Soviet Union would respect a neutral South-east Asia. The Thai view hovered somewhere in between, depending on the spokesman, but if Thanat Khoman's view is taken to be central, Thailand found the idea attractive in principle but, like Indonesia, wanted to see national self-reliance and regional co-operation working first. She suspected that a weak zone of neutrality would not last long, whereas a zone internally strong enough to withstand regional pressures and external domination might; in other words, she wanted armed, not unarmed, neutrality. The reaction of the external powers has been mixed, tending to be cool. The United States has shown no interest; the Soviet Union has shown interest but has been concerned to push her own elaborate proposal; China has blown hot and cold, and Japan has been non-committal.[60]

However, most new ideas arouse resistance at first and take time to implement. In the seven or eight years during which the Malaysian proposal has been under discussion, several developments have taken place which make it more attractive and some of the early scepticism about it less compelling:

(a) It was said at one time that the United States would want to maintain a strategic position in Thailand and could not, therefore, support neutrality. She does not now hold that position. It is said that the United States will want to keep a strategic position in the Philippines and cannot therefore agree to neutrality. But lately we have seen in the Philippines a tendency towards a more non-aligned position,[61] as she has cultivated relations with both China and the Soviet Union. If 'national control' of Subic Bay and Clark Field is given to the Philippines as a result of the current negotiations with the United States over the status of the bases, perhaps with gradual American withdrawal from the bases, the Philippines might become acceptably neutral. As can be seen from those now attending conferences of the non-aligned movement, the definition of neutrality is flexible.

(b) It is said that the Soviet Union and China will not agree on *anything*. But they may agree on *something*, if that something has the support of all the states of South-east Asia and does not offer benefits to either China or the Soviet Union to the disadvantage of the other.

(c) It is said that Vietnam cannot be trusted to honour any agreement (after her treatment of the Paris Treaties). This may have been a shrewd judgment of Vietnam while the country was still divided, when Hanoi had a clear view of its interests and pursued them single-mindedly. But the evidence since 1975 is that Hanoi has been pragmatic and realistic about its foreign relations. It is true that good intentions in politics are always subject to proof; nevertheless, Hanoi would enter the arrangement only after an examination of the benefits. The main benefits to Hanoi would be time and non-interference while the task of economic recovery and development is undertaken.

Yet Vietnam probably remains an obstacle, in the sense that she may not wish to give up her newly gained freedom as an actor in regional, and perhaps world, affairs by entering into arrangements with the ASEAN states. This draws attention to a weakness of the ZOPFAN proposal, which is the issue of whether its proposed region of neutrality would include all of South-east Asia (the ASEAN states as well as Burma, the Indo-China states and perhaps Papua New Guinea) or whether it would comprise only the ASEAN states, or indeed not all of them.[62] Some members of South-east Asia are firmly committed to the view that the whole region must be treated as a unity.[63] But if so, progress, if any, is likely to be slow, and the danger of conflict, during a period when the influence of the external powers is in abeyance, remains.

The central question of whether neutrality for South-east Asia is realistic may need to be looked at again, especially by Kuala Lumpur, in the light of the shift of power to Vietnam and subsequent developments in the region. If ASEAN continues to support neutrality, something more precise than the present well-meaning declaration of principle may be needed if the proposal is to be taken seriously. A common criticism of the present proposal, for example, is that it is pre-occupied with South-east Asian integrity and is unrealistic in expecting to exclude external influences. This is a criticism directed at other proposals for 'zones of peace', such as that for the Indian Ocean. However, while it may be unrealistic for South-east Asian states to try to *exclude* external influences (which, in any case, they do not really wish to do), it is perhaps not unrealistic for them to hope to *regulate* the influence of the external powers. Three areas of influence by external powers would call for particular attention:

(1) Alliances, bases and military arrangements. The five-power arrangements for Malaysia and Singapore would have to be phased out, as would the American presence in the Philippines. The latter would be a severe test of what the United States has stated to be a 'vital' interest. The case for holding on to bases can always be made to seem more substantial than it later appears (e.g. the American case for the Thai bases): how important for the United States are Subic Bay and Clark Field, compared with

Guam or Hawaii, especially if the Indian Ocean is not intended to become an area of increasing deployment?[64]

The notion of regional neutrality, as distinct from that of a single country, does raise difficult questions of defence and foreign policy, which would remain basically under the command of individual countries. It is likely that some military 'arrangements', as distinct from 'alliances', could continue with outside powers; for example, the provision of equipment and the sharing of intelligence. It need not be supposed that a neutral South-east Asia would create a local arms industry, servicing all indigenous countries with uniforms, weapons and equipment, nor that it would introduce a joint intelligence operation.

(b) Economic influence, such as is feared from Japan. Japan is planning to increase her trade, aid and investment in South-east Asia into the 1980s. The problem is deep-seated, for South-east Asia needs capital, and it is complicated by the fact that not all South-east Asian governments agree on the disadvantages of Japanese economic influence. The close links between Japanese business and government is as likely to be resented by Japan's business competitors as by host governments. Also, the consumer society which Japanese products help to create in South-east Asia is seen by some government leaders as a means of satisfying needs, discouraging dissent and maintaining themselves in power. Japan is herself aware of the hostility her economic penetration has aroused, but whether she will change course (so that, for example, agricultural and infrastructual aid and investment, which are not in the area where profits are made, are given more attention) is another matter.

(c) Subversion, externally supported. This contingency is possible within the region (e.g. Vietnam in Laos or Laos in Thailand; Indonesia in Borneo, during the period of confrontation with Malaysia; Indonesia in Timor), but its resolution would have to be left to 'consultation and co-operation' among the South-east Asians themselves. Outside the region the main concern is China. China's penetration of South-east Asia is cultural and ideological, which makes revolutionary guerrilla warfare an effective instrument for her. She can warn local governments about the 'big bad super-powers', but what can she offer them as an inducement to stay away from the Soviet Union and the United States? China's primitive aid programmes, while effective, do not appeal to nationalist leaders as much as state-sector aid from the Soviet Union or American private-sector aid. Both the Soviet Union and the United States wield more influence in the world than does China. China's main influence over the governments of South-east Asia is the threat she holds over them of subverting their authority or, conversely, of *not* harming them. This would be lost if China were to agree not to support subversion.

However, as has been suggested earlier in this paper (see pp. 16-17) this may be too simple a view of China's practical interest in South-east Asia. It cannot be supposed that China or any other external power could be prevented from supporting rebel or dissident groups in every sense at all times. Already China has herself made a distinction between ideological and material support. Also, China's attitude to South-east Asia is relaxed, as it is perceived through the experience of centuries. Provided no other power is establishing a dominant position in South-east Asia, China can reasonably assume that the region is benign. In particular, Peking's concern that the United States should not vacate the field for the Soviet Union gives it an interest, however complex, in the stability of governments well disposed to the United States. It is possible, taking these points into account, to see a neutral South-east Asia as attractive to China as a means of stabilizing the region. The deflation of insurgency, without its abandonment in principle, could be a price worth paying.

26

The shadow of Vietnam still falls across the path of American foreign policy in South-east Asia, so that terms like 'stability' and 'security' are challenged more than usual by the question: 'whose?' Recognition that her Vietnam policy failed has been muted for the United States by the demands of her friends in the region that she should not behave like a defeated power, by China's invitation to wait around, by her own interests in South-east Asia and by her slowly growing understanding that she can no longer revive the idyll of isolationism. At the time of writing, it is still too early to be sure what American security policy in South-east Asia will be, except that it will be more modest than in the past. But it is evident that if the United States were again to try to take an active interest in the security of South-east Asia, there would be a critical response from Moscow and Hanoi. Even without such an active interest, Moscow and Hanoi are ready to point an accusing finger at Washington, as shown by the attacks on continued Thai military links with the United States and allegations that Australia and Japan are trying to turn ASEAN into a military bloc at America's behest, as a successor to SEATO.[65] Any suggestion – even one which is politically self-interested, as in the case of Moscow and Hanoi – that a military policy is contemplated by the United States or her allies, not only arouses sensitivities in the ASEAN group but is also unwelcome in Japan and Australia, where public opinion remains suspicious of military commitments in South-east Asia and official opinion is, at least, ambiguous.

While there is obviously, therefore, a need for a fresh approach to the security of South-east Asia (and fragmentary evidence of this is beginning to emerge),[66] progress has been slow. Even – perhaps especially – on the Communist side, security questions are raised and pursued in traditional military-ideological manner. The momentum of this debate will lead to division and conflict, not reconciliation, and although some non-Communist leaders of South-east Asia may see short-term political advantages in confrontation, the long-term interest of non-Communist South-east Asia lies in reconciliation.

The question at the heart of South-east Asia's security is whether Vietnam is nationalist or Communist or – to restate the issue more realistically, as Vietnam is obviously both nationalist and Communist – whether Vietnam will act as an agent of revolution in South-east Asia alone or in association with either the Soviet Union or China or both, or will accept, perhaps even encourage, a non-Communist ASEAN as a source of independent strength and support for herself in her relations with her big Communist brothers. The parallel with Yugoslavia which some propose is not entirely apt. Yugoslavia has an overwhelming Soviet presence to contend with, while Vietnam has to contend with China and is using the Soviet Union as a counterweight. This gives her more room to manoeuvre than Yugoslavia. Also, Vietnam has a strategic interest in Laos and an ancient rivalry with Cambodia, both of which extend her concern with security beyond her borders and provide her with options to use against the Communist giants.

Vietnam also has a more exposed and valuable coastline than Yugoslavia, giving her a strategic position on the trade routes of the South China Sea, facing Taiwan, the Philippines and eastern Malaysia. All these factors suggest, as do her comparative size and strength, that Vietnam will be more active in her neighbourhood than Yugoslavia is – she will be a regional power, in other words, rather than a chip held delicately in an East–West balance. However, while it is too early to be confident about the kind of security outlook Vietnam will adopt, her nationalistic history, the uniqueness of her revolution and her pragmatic behaviour since the end of the War suggest that a Vietnamese role in the region need not threaten the ASEAN states. Indeed, if the earlier analysis of this paper is correct and the test of the stability of non-Communist South-east Asia is more likely to be social and political than military, acceptance of Vietnam, in the form of a local detente, would be of more help to the ASEAN states than exclusion of Vietnam and a crusade against Communism at home.

At present the ASEAN countries are closely linked with the advanced industrial states and there is a strong disposition, in both the industrial states and ASEAN, to see any change from the present forms of government as a threat to stability, because it would threaten existing investment, commercial and trading patterns. Similarly, in Laos, Cambodia and Vietnam peaceful change from now on will occur, if it occurs at all, only if initiated at the top. Thus the prospects for peaceful social and political change in the region are slight. In both cases the response to pressures for change is likely to be repression. Some observers already see the ASEAN states as on the treadmill of highly capitalized development, political repression, social stagnation and 'revolution' by coup and counter-coup which has characterized Latin America. The Indo-China states, while following different social and economic policies from each other, are squarely in the Communist tradition of centralized authority and the suppression of any alternative philosophy.

In more optimistic moments one wonders whether this is not too harsh a picture. For one thing, South-east Asia benefits from uncommon qualities of leadership. The combination of religion, race and colonial experience, and the need, for reasons of trade and commerce, to keep up with world politics, have produced strong and competent leadership as varied as the names of Abdul Rahman, Ho Chi Minh, Lee Kuan Yew, Magsaysay, Marcos, Ngo Dinh Diem, Sihanouk, Suharto, Sukarno and U Nu suggest. For another, the states of South-east Asia, with a few exceptions, have been cautious about aligning themselves fully with the political and military strategy of the West and may be cautious now about others' global economic and political strategies. Also, unlike the Latin American countries, South-east Asia has four great powers to play with. The region has other options than being for or against one dominant power.

The danger exists, however. It is significant that no notable leadership has emerged in Thailand, where a succession of military leaders have taken their country closest to the Latin American model without winning popular support. It is also true that while the economies of South-east Asia have been resilient, they are still heavily dependent on commodity prices. In the last ten years the ASEAN countries profited from the Vietnam War and spent little on defence themselves. The future could be more demanding, and some leaders may feel they cannot survive without becoming associated even more

closely than at present with the industrial states. This applies especially to their commercial links, and particularly to their links with the United States and Japan, while the Australian connection is also increasing in significance. A quasi-formal link between ASEAN and Japan, Australia and New Zealand was established in August 1977 when, after a meeting of ASEAN heads of government in Kuala Lumpur, discussions were held with the prime ministers of these three non-ASEAN countries. On this occasion Australia, pleading inflation and unemployment, was unmoved by ASEAN's request for greater access to the Australian market – a foretaste of ASEAN's problem in trying to find an economic factor of stability during a period of uncertainty in the capitalist system.[67]

In other words, a locked-in adversary relationship with Vietnam, while it would simplify internal politics in the ASEAN countries in the short run, could also place a strain on economic and social developments in non-Communist South-east Asia, which is at present static rather than stable, brittle rather than strong. Whether outsiders can assist stability is doubtful. They require stable conditions for investment, but their assistance is likely to be counter-productive in a situation of tension, once the cycle of foreign dependence, nationalist resentment and Communist insurgency becomes established.

Insurgency has deep roots in South-east Asia and utopianism a respected place in its folklore. As Communism is a revolutionary doctrine, Communist states can be expected to continue to promote Communism outside their borders. The ASEAN states must prepare to deal, therefore, with revolutionary terrorism and guerrilla warfare, which are facts in South-east Asia, not fictions of anti-Communist imaginations. But they can do so with the knowledge, which was neglected in the American crusade against Vietnam, that there are several kinds of Communism and that Communist states are selective about their support for revolutions. China, in particular, has shown that nothing in her revolutionary doctrine requires her materially to assist Communist-led rebels who cannot themselves hope to prevail. As the Communist rebels in ASEAN countries look mainly to the Soviet Union and China for support or, if they are urban intellectuals, find their inspiration in

28

Euro-Communism, the ASEAN governments would gain a psychological advantage by promoting good relations with Vietnam, the newest and most admired Communist state – and South-east Asian as well. The worst approach is an undifferentiated anti-Communism, which dramatizes the strength of Communism, obscures its differences and raises internal tension within the non-Communist societies. A more flexible approach will require adjustments in the thinking of ASEAN leaders, but in a direction they have been moving towards for some time: national and regional 'self-reliance' and 'resilience' are phrases which describe inadequately a process of growing away from colonial ties and cold war dependencies. A productive accommodation with Vietnam would be an important additional step.

The conflict between capitalism and Communism has been shown in South-east Asia not to lead to stability, as it has in Europe (although at the cost of great military confrontation), so it would seem wise for political leaders who need stability to turn away from security arrangements which are based on such a conflict. This is an important issue for the United States, Japan and Australia also, not because they might be contemplating new security arrangements, which is improbable, but because their influence in South-east Asia has been associated with shoring up local societies against Communism. This has distorted their own foreign policies – Japan's much less – and has provoked a running battle with their South-east Asian friends on the issue of 'human rights', the serious infringements being usually in the cause of anti-Communism. A broader outlook in the ASEAN capitals, based on expanding relations with Vietnam, would discourage paranoia in Washington and Canberra, not to mention Moscow and Hanoi, and would encourage the diversity and variety in which democracy can grow.[68]

CONCLUSION

Some general observations about South-east Asian security can be stated more explicitly:

(1) No power or group of powers, whether the combination is external or regional or both, can expect to dominate South-east Asia in peacetime. This is partly the result of the present divided nature of the area – a power or combination of powers that might expect to dominate mainland South-east Asia would be resisted by another power or combination of powers in the archipelago states – but it is also an effect of the checks and balances applied by the external powers to each other. None of them is disposed to allow others to dominate South-east Asia. It sometimes appears that China and Japan would be prepared to allow the United States to do so, and in the case of Japan this is probably true at present. However, it may be true only so far as the conservatives continue to hold power in Tokyo, and even in conservative circles there is a wariness about relying on the United States. In addition, enticements for the United States to 'stay' in South-east Asia must be assessed against a background of American unwillingness, after Vietnam, to give South-east Asia a high priority. A plea for the United States not to go too far away is different from asking her to take a dominant role.

It is sometimes said that Japan and China, because they are Asian powers, have 'natural' rights in South-east Asia. This is not the view of the region itself. Japan's right to a 'sphere of influence' in South-east Asia is not taken seriously, even in Japan, while she has no external military capability. Economic dominance is possible but, as already noted, this would expose Japan's political and military weakness. A view that Chinese influence is more acceptable now in South-east Asia than that of other external powers is not borne out by the attitudes of Djakarta and Hanoi, nor by the suspicion of Chinese minorities by South-east Asia's ethnic majorities. The commercial nature of South-east Asia's links with the outside world and its importance as an international thoroughfare would make Chinese dominance difficult, although a slow growth of benign Chinese influence can be expected.

(2) The position of Singapore and Malaysia as the pivots of the former British security arrangements, and of Thailand and the Philippines as mainstays of an American presence, can no longer be maintained. The two most important countries, which were excluded from the security arrangements for the region in the 1950s and 1960s, are Indonesia and Vietnam. These are stronger and more ambitious states than the four which provided the basis for Anglo-American hegemony, with a correspondingly less pliant attitude to outsiders.

(3) The main guarantee of peace in South-east Asia, as in the Asia–Pacific region generally, lies in the absence of conflict between the four powers, the United States, the Soviet Union, China and Japan. If conflict or rivalry between these four powers becomes intense, South-east Asia will suffer as the great powers move and manoeuvre in the pursuit of major interests to which South-east Asia is peripheral. On the other hand, conflict between South-east Asian states, if unattended by the great powers, is unlikely to affect the stability of the region as a whole. South-east Asia thus has a stake in the success of detente between the United States and the Soviet Union, in accommodation between the United States and China, and in the satisfaction of Japan's economic and political interests without conflict. On the evidence of its history and its geopolitical situation, South-east Asia cannot insulate itself from great-power relationships.

These observations point to continued great-power involvement in South-east Asia without, however, indicating how this will or can contribute to its security. It is difficult at present to see how new forms of security can emerge, if these would require military arrangements with the great powers, yet it is also plain that the dream of some South-east Asian nationalists, that everything would be fine if the external powers were removed, is not about to be realized either. The essence of the security question is that no counter exists to the power, actual and potential, of Vietnam, which is indisputably South-east Asian and nationalist. A counter is needed because her fellow South-east Asians have based themselves on non-Communist, even anti-Communist, forms of society which they fear, in the absence of their protectors, they will not now be able to sustain.

Time is needed for the ASEAN states, especially Indonesia, to become accustomed to the shift of power to Vietnam and to make more precise assessments of the kind of threat, if any, Vietnam offers to the stability of South-east Asia. If an organization for Asia existed on the model of the Organization of African Unity (OAU) or the Organization of American States (OAS) it would no doubt be the forum for discussion of ways of reconciling the new Vietnam with the old South-east Asia but, significantly, no such organization exists. There are probably too many powers in Asia. The OAU works because it excludes only a few African states whereas many important Asian states might have to be excluded from any Asian organization. The OAS works because there is only one dominating power (the United States) whereas there might be too many states of the second rank attempting to dominate any Asian organization. Proposals for something even as loose as an Asia – Pacific forum by leaders like Mr Whitlam and Mrs Gandhi have foundered on the issue of who, indeed, is in Asia, let alone 'Asian', and Mr Brezhnev's collective security proposal for Asia has been coolly received, partly because of suspicion of Soviet motives, but partly because it is being promoted by a power whose claim to be 'Asian' is no greater than that, say, of the United States.

Time may be available. Vietnam has a long task of rehabilitation and reconstruction ahead and has problems to attend to in her relations with the Soviet Union, China and Cambodia. The future of Thailand could severely test relations between Vietnam and the ASEAN states but the issue has been raised too soon after the Vietnam War to stimulate genuine interest in an anti-Communist common front on Thailand's behalf. The process of disintegration in Thailand is likely to be slow. While the case for a classic neutrality is hard to make in present circumstances in South-east Asia, a mixture of the two options discussed in Chapter VIII could emerge in time, as the ASEAN states become more confident that, in the absence of external powers, they can reach a *modus vivendi* with Vietnam. The outcome could be a novel form of detente.

European detente began as the essentially strategic concept of two super-powers, whose armed forces, with those of their allies, divide Europe. South-east Asian detente would be more complex. It would be intra-regional, requiring an understanding essentially between Vietnam and Indonesia, but it would also require a form of detente between the four external powers, either formal or tacit, that they would not interfere militarily within the region. A model could be the Chinese anti-hegemony clause, which is directed against the Soviet Union but could be adapted by the South-east Asians for use against all the external powers. Probably, however, a process will emerge by trial and error, as it did in Europe, requiring pressures from within (such as the efforts of Willy Brandt) as well as calculations from without. South-east Asia is well sited for the test, as it is an area where the four powers have almost equal status, although differing widely in their respective economic, political and military weight. This gives a kind of unity, if largely diplomatic, to their presence and to their acknowledgment of each other. It is also an area where local diversity is strong. The popular slogan 'unity in diversity', which is useful to cover situations where an enforced unity would mean no unity at all, would apply, in the sense that if the external powers were unified in their disposition not to take up dominant positions in the region – and the analysis of this paper suggests that their interests do not stand in the way of such consensus – variety and diversity in South-east Asia, as well as stability, could be maintained. But it is, admittedly, a sophisticated idea and statesmanship, both inside and outside the region, is not noticeably active on its behalf at the present moment.

However, the absence of immediate answers may be reassuring, if we recall the lack of success of instant solutions in the past. The conditions for spectacular diplomacy are not present, and forcing the issue could be harmful. Although diplomacy could have an important role to play in the security of South-east Asia in the future, it must first encourage the right conditions – a 'balance of confidence' in the region, so that the states of South-east Asia do not fear each other, and a more deliberate appreciation by the external powers of the benefits of peaceful relations between themselves. The argument for time is not, therefore, an argument for leaving things alone. It is an argument for consciously encouraging a relaxation of tension in the belief that, calmly examined, the interests of states in the region and the powers outside it can be harmonized.

Other trouble spots are pre-occupying the great powers. Europe itself, the Middle East and southern Africa are more pressing, as are Korea and Taiwan in the Asia–Pacific region. Indeed, after a couple of decades on the front burner, South-east Asia sometimes seems to have been removed by many governments not to the back burner, but into cold storage. We can be sure, however, that it will not remain there indefinitely: both history and geography will see to that.

NOTES

[1] *The Miltary Balance* 1977-1978 (London: IISS, 1976), pp. 58–65.

[2] See reference to unavailability of spare parts in *International Herald Tribune,* November 1976.

[3] SEATO was dismantled on 30 June 1977, but signatories used the occasion to note that they remained parties to the Manila Treaty, which would continue. The Australian Government, for example, said the Treaty remained 'an expression of the determination of member states that the countries of this region should be free to determine their own destinies and plan their own futures free from outside interference'. The Manila Treaty is important to Thailand which, unlike the Philippines, has no other security treaty with the United States. Article IV, Paragraph 1, states that each party will, in the event of aggression by means of armed attack in the treaty area, 'act to meet the common danger in accordance with its constitutional processes'. Paragraph 2 states that the parties 'shall consult immediately in order to agree on the measures which should be taken for the common defence'.

[4] Examined in Chapter VIII.

[5] The difficulties in applying 'balance of power' concepts to Asia are examined by Coral Bell in *The Asian Balance of Power: A Comparison with European Precedents,* Adelphi Paper No. 44 (London: IISS, 1968). See also Michio Royama, *The Asian Balance of Power: A Japanese View,* Adelphi Paper No. 42 (London: IISS, 1967).

[6] Official English text of Address to the Nation, 8 October 1976.

[7] *International Herald Tribune,* 10 December 1976.

[8] Quoted in BBC Summary of World Broadcasts (swb), 16 February 1977. A particular cause for further comment was a meeting in Thailand on 24 February of 'Special Forces' commanders from South Korea,

Singapore, the Philippines, the United States and Thailand. The American representative was Major-General Robert Kingston, who was reported by Hanoi to have appeared 'wearing his green beret and paratrooper boots' (swb, 26 February 1977). See also a Hanoi radio report that Thanat Khoman had claimed on 12 February that the 'old agreements' on the dispatch of American troops to Thailand were still valid (swb, 19 February 1977).

[9] This estimate does not include the students and intellectuals who joined after the October coup. Estimates of their numbers vary from a couple of hundred to a couple of thousand. For a well informed account, see Hamish McDonald, 'Thailand: an unstable government awaits a new strong man', *The National Times* (Sydney), 13 June 1977.

[10] See Robert Shaplen, 'Fragility in South-east Asia', *International Herald Tribune*, 13 January 1977. This figure was disputed by officials in Washington during a visit by the author in April 1977: they claimed it was too high.

[11] See McDonald, *op. cit.* in note 9.

[12] An unsuccessful coup by army officers in March 1977 was followed by an armed forces coup on 20 October 1977, after which the military assumed a more overt political role under the prime ministership of the Supreme Commander of the Armed Forces, General Kriangsak Chamanand. Some observers saw dissatisfaction with Thanin's handling of relations with Vietnam, Cambodia and Laos as one of the reasons for the coup, and early reactions to the coup by the Indo-Chinese Communist governments were encouraging.

[13] According to the Governor of Nakkon Phanom province, fighting between Laotian factions had spilled over into Thailand during March 1977. A 'battalion', now stationed on Thai territory, had been promoted to 'a government in exile'. He did not specify which faction was now in exile, nor what subversion it was perpetrating in Thailand, but the scenario is certainly plausible. Fighting between Thai and Cambodian soldiers over a disputed border village near Aranyprathet, east of Bangkok, took place in July 1977.

[14] A new Thai–Malaysian border agreement was signed on 4 March 1977. It provided for a combined task-force headquarters and 'combined, co-ordinated and unilateral' operations, the latter allowing independent action on the part of either Thai or Malaysian forces in the event of their wishing to cross the border in 'hot pursuit'. Both the Malaysian and Thai prime ministers have been anxious to assure their people that this does not mean a violation of sovereignty, which is the main point of propaganda against the agreement, especially by the 'Voice of the People of Thailand' (see swb, 8 March 1977). Publicity has been given by both Kuala Lumpur and Bangkok to renewed border-security activities, code-named 'Big Star-Destroy I' and 'Big Star-Destroy II' (see swb, 18 March 1977), although the results have been vaguely reported.

[15] Indonesia has increased its border-security activities in co-operation with Malaysia. An army spokesman told journalists on 1 March, 1977 that Indonesia was also considering joint military exercises with Malaysia.

If the exercise took place, it would be the first by the Indonesian army with a foreign country. (swb, 4 March 1977).

[16] See Malaysian Treasury Economic Report (Kuala Lumpur: Government Printer, 1974).

[17] For example, remarks on detente by the Defence Minister, General Panggabean, in an address to the armed forces (swb, 11 March 1977). The Indonesian Government, including both President Suharto and the Foreign Minister, Mr Adam Malik, have maintained that border-security operations within asean do not constitute a 'military alliance' because they are not directed against a 'foreign country' but against 'subversive elements' (swb, 1 March 1977).

[18] By late 1977 the flow of boat refugees was increasing, as were the distances travelled, causing problems for the governments in Australia, Korea and Japan. For a detailed account, see Robert Shaplen, 'A Reporter at Large', *The New Yorker,* 5 September 1977.

[19] See the argument of former Indonesian Minister for Finance, Sumitro Djojohadikusomo, in *Indonesia Towards the Year 2000* (Djakarta: Institute for Economic and Social Survey, University of Indonesia, 1975).

[20] Singapore's internal-security concern today is the English-educated youth, which reflects radical tendencies in Europe and the United States, rather than the Chinese-educated youth, which was its concern in the 1950s and 1960s. The much-discussed 'malaise' of Lee Kuan Yew's successful regime in Singapore is an English-language phenomenon.

[21] See, however, the charge by former Rector of Thammasat University, Bangkok, Dr Puey Ungphakorn, that Lee Kuan Yew wishes to fight the 'Communist threat' in Thailand rather than in Singapore (the *Age*, 12 July, 1977).

[22] The southern provinces of the Philippines – thirteen in number – have substantial numbers of Moslems and five have Moslem majorities. The Philippines is predominantly Catholic.

[23] Stockholm home service, 28 January 1977 (swb, 2 February 1977).

[24] Précis of Tanjug report from Tokyo on 6 January 1977, in swb, 16 February 1977.

[25] *International Herald Tribune*, 24 January 1977.

[26] New Delhi home service, 14 February 1977 (swb, 17 February 1977).

[27] Hanoi home service, 1 February 1977 (swb, 4 February 1977).

[28] *Nhan Dan,* 12 February 1977 (swb, 15 February 1977).

[29] *Nhan Dan,* 3 February 1977 (swb, 9 February 1977).

[30] It appears, however, that an attempt will be made to preserve Saigon's special character. See Hanoi home service, 4 February 1977 (swb, 7 February 1977) on its development as 'a big socialist commercial port and a centre of international communications and relations'.

[31] André Gelinas, 'Life in the New Vietnam', *New York Review*, 17 March 1977.

[32] For a contrast, see Gareth Porter, 'Vietnam's Long Road to Socialism', *Current History*, December, 1976, and Le Thi Tuyet, *Vietnam: Socialism in Search of Capital* (Georgetown: Centre for Strategic and International Studies, Georgetown University, 1976).

[33] *Nhan Dan*, 2 February 1977 (SWB, 9 February 1977) referred to national calamities, small-scale scattered production and low labour productivity in an editorial on food shortages. An article in the March 1977 issue of *Tap Chi Cong San*, reported by Hanoi radio, said that Vietnam's population was increasing too rapidly for economic development and improved living standards. At the present rate of 3 per cent annual growth, the population would be 100 million by the year 2000 (SWB, 25 March 1977).

[34] See Kenneth M. Quinn, 'Cambodia 1976: Internal Consolidation and External Expansion', *Asian Survey*, Vol. 17, No. I, January 1977. The existence of the Kampuchean Communist Party (KCP) was publicly revealed at a mass meeting in Phnom Penh on 27 September 1977. Before that it had simply been known as the Revolutionary Organization. The KCP Secretary and Prime Minister of Democratic Kampuchea is Pol Pot, but the name is widely believed to be a pseudonym of Khmer Communist leader, Saloth Sar. Why there was such delay in acknowledging the KCP is unclear.

[35] For an account of 'a suicide of a people in the name of revolution' see a review article by Jean Lacouture (of François Ponchaud, *Cambodge. Année Zero*), 'The Bloodiest Revolution', in the *New York Review of Books*, 31 March 1977, p. 9.

[36] The tone of Phnom Penh radio's comments was noticeably emotional in rejecting the American Woodcock delegation: 'The Cambodian people have always respected and liked progressive Americans . . . with regard to the US imperialists, our Cambodian people will never forget their acts of aggression . . . The national and class anger of the Cambodian people [is] . . . still boiling . . . An immense number of bitter experiences – felt through their flesh, blood and bones – at the hand of the US imperialists . . .' (SWB, 21 March 1977).

[37] Pol Pot visited China and Korea in September-October 1977, on his first visit overseas as Prime Minister. He was received at the highest level in Peking. It was revealed during the visit that he had made a secret journey to Peking in June 1975 and had met the late Chairman Mao.

[38] Laos virtually existed on American aid and Western financial backing for her currency in the 1950s and 1960s. Now she has become dependent on Vietnam and Soviet help. Being landlocked, she is also dependent on the goodwill of her neighbours; for example Soviet tractors and trailers sent as aid had to receive transit permission from Thailand (SWB, 14 February 1977). In July 1977 a twenty-five-year Treaty of Friendship and Co-operation was signed with Vietnam. Vietnam has also opened a highway into Laos from her port in Danang, where goods destined for Laos will be given priority. See Carlyle A. Thayer, 'Vietnam in World Affairs', in *Dyason House Papers*, Vol. 3, No. 5, 1977 (Melbourne: Australian Institute of International Affairs).

[39] Leslie H. Brown, *American Security Policy in Asia*, Adelphi Paper No. 132 (London: IISS, 1977), pp. 7–8.

[40] Testimony by Richard Holbrooke to the House of Representatives' Committee on International Relations, official text, 10 March 1977.

[41] According to official Japanese figures, at the end of 1975 Japan was the biggest investor in Thailand, Malaysia and Indonesia, and in ASEAN as a whole. Japanese exports to the region (about 10 per cent of her exports) have not grown during the last decade, but imports have increased (from about 9 to 12 per cent). The overall importance of Japan to the ASEAN group is that she accounts for 25–30 per cent of its trade (both ways) and is by far its largest trading partner.

[42] A critical view of Japan is taken by Raul S. Manglapus in 'Japan in South-east Asia: Collision Course' (New York: Carnegie Endowment for International Peace, 1976). He describes the combination of 'power and vulnerability' in Japan's role as 'particularly flammable'. Japan's international role remains the subject of intense debate within Japan. Kei Wakaizumi analyses 'positivist' and 'passivist' tendencies in 'Japan's Dilemma: To Act or Not to Act', *Foreign Policy*, No. 16, Fall 1974.

[43] China's share of ASEAN exports in 1974 was 0.8 per cent and of imports, 3.1 per cent.

[44] See, for example, comments by General Ali Murtopo on difficulties in restoring relations with Peking. He referred to problems of Indonesians of Chinese ancestry and relations between Peking and Indonesian communists (Djakarta home service, SWB, 8 February 1977).

[45] The Soviet Union's share of the ASEAN countries' trade in 1974 was 1.6 per cent of their exports and 0.2 per cent of their imports.

[46] Formal agreements between the Burmese Communist Party, the Kachen Independence Movement and the Shan State People's Liberation Army were announced in January 1977 (SWB, February 1 1977).

[47] In fact, Ne Win came to power as a consequence of the threat to state integrity posed by the separatists (see Michael Leifer, *Dilemmas of Statehood in South-east Asia* (Vancouver: University of British Columbia, 1972), p. 18.

[48] The Burmese army has managed to contain the BCP in the Shan state between the Salween River and the Chinese border. China has provided sanctuary, training and material. In November 1976 the chairman of the BCP, Thakin Ba Thein Tin, led a delegation to Peking where he was received by Hua Kuo-feng in his capacity as chairman of the Chinese Communist Party.

[49] Early in 1977 signs of unrest in the Burmese army and the Burmese Socialist Programme Party (BSPP) suggested that Ne Win's leadership might be challenged. However, he consolidated his position at the Party Congress in November 1977, after the release of the first detailed official statement on the fighting. The release said that 500 BCP guerrillas and 126 Burmese soldiers had been killed in heavy fighting on the border during October, when a BCP force of 1,500 men tried to gain control of a strategic highway. Ne Win then promptly paid visits to China and Kampuchea (where his visit was the first by a head of state since the Khmer Rouge victory in 1975). During 1977 Ne Win showed interest in a closer association with the ASEAN states and Japan.

[50] For details, including minimum width and depth, of straits and channels in the Asia-Pacific area, see

appendices to T. B. Millar, 'The Indian and Pacific Oceans: Some Strategic Considerations', Adelphi Paper No. 57 (London: IISS, 1969).

[51] An agreement on shipping rules in the Malacca Straits was signed on 24 February 1977 by Indonesia Malaysia and Singapore. It excludes vessels of more than 20,000 tons. According to Indonesia's Foreign Minister, Mr Adam Malik, an agreement on the passage of warships would be concluded later. The *People's Daily* welcomed the agreement as a 'telling blow' to Soviet 'maritime hegemony' (SWB, 15 March 1977).

[52] See report in the *New York Times*, 7 February 1977.

[53] For a detailed discussion, see Barry Buzan, 'The New Asian Regime: Sources of Dispute', forthcoming Adelphi Paper.

[54] See 'Asia's Jugular Straits: the Unsolved Problem', *Far Eastern Economic Review*, Vol. 95, No. 6, 11 February 1977.

[55] The Ombai-Wetar Straits are north of Timor. It was reported that the United States warned the Australian government not to allow a deterioration of relations with Djakarta on the Timor issue, as Indonesian goodwill was needed for the passage of submarines (see the *Age* (Melbourne), 3 August 1976).

[56] Robert E. Osgood, 'Military Implications of the New Ocean Regime', in *Power at Sea: Part I: The New Environment*, Adelphi Paper No. 122 (London: IISS, 1976), p. 14.

[57] See, for example, Wolfgang Stargardt, 'Neutrality and Neutralization in South-east Asia', in Dahm and Draguhn, eds, *Politics, Society and Economy in the ASEAN States* (Wiesbaden: Harrassowitz, 1975).

[58] A good account of the Malaysian proposal and some general discussion of various concepts is given by Dick Wilson in *The Neutralisation of South-east Asia* (New York: Praeger, 1975).

[59] The wording of the Kuala Lumpur Declaration, 27 November 1971, signed by Indonesia, Malaysia, the Philippines, Singapore and Thailand.

[60] Attitudes of the different South-east Asian states and external powers are dealt with in detail in Wilson, *op. cit.* in note 58, Parts II and III.

[61] See an interview with President Marcos by Henry Kamm, *International Herald Tribune*, 25 February 1977.

[62] Wolfgang Stargardt, 'Neutrality within the Asian System of Powers', in Lauk Teik Soon, ed., *New Directions in the International Relations of South-East Asia* (Singapore: University Press, 1973). The suggestion is made here that Indonesia is too strong an actor to find neutrality attractive.

[63] For example, Soedjatmoko, 'The Role of the Medium and Small Nations in the New Asia–Pacific Setting', in *Foreign Policy for Australia: Choices for the 70s* (Sydney: Australian Institute of Political Science, 1973): 'The only hope for a relatively stable South-east Asia region, free from external-power interference, lies in the adoption of the concept of a single South-east Asia, a region of South-east Asian co-operation encompassing the whole of South-east Asia, including Indo-China and specifically including North Vietnam.'

[64] For a reported view within the United States State Department in favour of American withdrawal from bases in the Philippines, see the *Wall Street Journal*, 10 March 1977.

[65] See the criticism by the Soviet armed forces daily, *Red Star*, reported in the *Age* (Melbourne), 31 July 1977.

[66] The communique of the ANZUS Council meeting in Wellington, New Zealand, 28 July 1977, showed a movement of emphasis from military to economic factors in security.

[67] Australia's attitude to South-east Asia has undergone a change which is still taking shape. Forward defence was abandoned after the Vietnam *débacle*, and the election of a Labour government in 1972. With the return of a conservative government in 1975, concern was expressed about the influence of the Soviet Union in the Asia–Pacific area, especially the Indian Ocean, but no changes in policy could be detected. Although a 'two-tier' policy, separating mainland and archipelago, has been favourably considered by Defence and Foreign Affairs officials for some time, the conservative government, like its Labour predecessors, publicly supported accommodation between the ASEAN and Indo-China Communist states. However, in what was described as a 'personal and confidential' letter which found its way into the press, Foreign Minister Peacock wrote to Secretary of State Vance on 31 August 1977, urging more American attention to South-east Asia in order to check Vietnamese dominance and relieve pressure on Japan to play a role. See the *Australian Financial Review*, 3, 4 and 5 October 1977.

[68] This theme is developed on a global basis by Stanley Hoffman in 'No Choice, No Illusions', *Foreign Policy*, No. 25, Winter 1976–77. In particular, the argument that critics of capitalism should not be regarded as dupes of Moscow and that the United States should stress 'equality' as well as 'liberty' are relevant to the situation in South-east Asia.

ADELPHI PAPERS

The following is a selection of those available. They may be ordered from the Institute at a current price of **50p ($1.50)** *per copy, post free by surface mail (air mail prices on application).*

Discount rates are available for bulk orders of 11 or more Adelphi Papers of the same title.

Printed in Great Britain by LSG Printers, Portland Street, Lincoln.

ADELPHI PAPERS
NUMBER ONE HUNDRED AND FORTY-TWO

The Security of South-East Asia

by Bruce Grant

THE INTERNATIONAL INSTITUTE FOR STRATEGIC STUDIES
18 ADAM STREET LONDON WC2N 6AL

ADELPHI PAPER NO. 142

Bruce Grant, writer and scholar, has written widely on Asian affairs and was Australian High Commissioner in India 1973–6. He undertook the work for this Paper while a Research Associate at the IISS in 1977.

First published Spring 1978

ISBN O 86079 017 7
ISSN 0567–932X

The International Institute for Strategic Studies was founded in 1958 as a centre for the provision of information on and research into the problems of international security, defence and arms control in the nuclear age. It is international in its Council and staff, and its membership is drawn from over fifty countries. It is independent of governments and is not the advocate of any particular interest.

The Institute is concerned with strategic questions – not just with the military aspects of security but with the social and economic sources and political and moral implications of the use and existence of armed force: in other words, with the basic problems of peace.

The Institute's publications are intended for a much wider audience than its own membership and are available to the general public on subscription or singly.